The

BOOMERS' GUIDE

to

ONLINE DATING

RODALE

LIVE YOUR WHOLE LIFE™

Every day our brands
connect with and inspire
millions of people to live
a life of the mind, body,
spirit — a whole life.

DATE WITH DIGNITY

The

BOOMERS' GUIDE

to

ONLINE DATING

JUDSEN CULBRETH

RODALE

Author's note on profiles and stories:
Online couples that agreed to let me use their real names are identified by first and last names. I've changed the first name and some identifying details of those who wished to be anonymous or those whose stories were posted online without last names. Profiles are real, but have been edited. A few are composites. I've changed identifying details, although almost all of them probably have been taken off the sites for some time.

© 2005 by Judsen Culbreth
Cover Photographs © 2005 by Rodale Inc.

Printed in the United States of America
Rodale Inc. makes every effort to use acid-free ∞ recycled paper ♻.

Book design by Tara Long

Library of Congress Cataloging-in-Publication Data
Culbreth, Judsen.
    The boomers' guide to online dating / Judsen Culbreth.
        p.   cm.
    Includes bibliographical references and index.
    ISBN-13 978–1–59486–225–0 paperback
    ISBN-10 1–59486–225–7 paperback
    1. Online dating.   2. Baby boom generation.   3. Mate selection.   I. Title.
    HQ801.82.C84   2005
    646.7'7'028546780844—dc22   2005008336

Distributed to the trade by Holtzbrinck Publishers

2 4 6 8 10 9 7 5 3 1 paperback

RODALE
LIVE YOUR WHOLE LIFE™

We inspire and enable people to improve their lives and the world around them
For more of our products visit rodalestore.com or call 800-848-4735

TO WALTER, MY #1 MATCH

DELIGHT YOURSELF IN THE LORD, AND HE WILL
GIVE YOU THE DESIRES OF YOUR HEART.

—PSALMS 37:4

CONTENTS

ACKNOWLEDGMENTS

I would like to thank Stephanie Tade of Rodale Books and my agent, Susan Ginsburg of Writers House, for their unwavering belief in this project. My editor, Jennifer Kushnier, followed through on her promise: "We can conquer anything together."

Bob Smithers and his team at Moss Warner Communications provided valuable help early on by coming up with the clever cover for the proposal and Maggie Lovaas for the formatting. Photographer Chuck Fishman not only created an extraordinary chronicle of my wedding day, but also was kind enough to let me use a favorite photo on the back cover. Tom Becker provided copyediting assistance with the proposal. Joyce Williams supplied hard-to-find academic papers.

My friends and family have been patient and supportive through every stage. Kathy and Dave Vogel were especially nice to offer me a quiet place to work and a running supply of iced tea and sandwiches in the final deadline days. I owe a special thanks to Kate White, Jan Harayda, and my friends in publishing who've been so generous with professional advice and contacts.

Finally, I am most grateful to the online daters who shared the stories of finding their soul mates and to Becky Swanston, who talked Walter into trying online dating.

INTRODUCTION

The bank officer was an attractive, well-dressed woman in her early 50s. As she input my application for a new checking account, she asked about my employment. I told her I was writing a book.

"May I ask what it's about?" she said, smiling.

I told her I'd met my husband online, and the book's goal was to encourage and help other mature daters. Her professional demeanor did a 180.

"My God, when's it coming out?" she whispered. "I haven't had a date in 15 years."

For the nearly 16 million single women ages 35 to 64, dating can be daunting. You may be one of them. Experienced about life, you may feel oddly naive when it comes to romance. After all, you're not in a stage of development, like the high school years to late 20s, when dating is the natural social thing to do. You may have been married for decades—most of your friends still probably are—and the thought of new relationships makes you feel vulnerable, even though you yearn for the chance to love again.

Maybe you're reluctant to give dating a chance because you've heard that there are no available men your age. Don't believe it. Statistics turn up 1.4 single Boomer women for every unmarried Boomer man. Not bad odds—a savvy single Boomer woman only has to beat out half a person. When you look at another important ripple of mature daters—13 million singles ages 35 to 44—men outnumber women by 6 percent.

So the statistics aren't anywhere near as awful as you suspected. What may be discouraging, however, is the inability to connect with those millions of prospective daters. The men are there in volume, but you haven't found even one. I know how that goes from personal experience.

When I found myself single again at age 49, after a 20-year marriage, I expected my large cheering squad of friends and acquaintances to fix me up. And they tried. Net: two blind dates in two years. I had about equal luck on my own, hoping for a fateful meeting.

Then, while at a brunch for professional women, I eavesdropped on a conversation that changed my life. Two women were comparing notes about the men they'd met through online dating. I decided to give this new way of dating a try.

Two days after posting on an Internet dating site and asking for matches within a 50-mile radius of Manhattan, I had 84 responses. Over the next year, I posted my profile on six sites. I screened thousands of men, corresponded with more than 100 of them, and liked 25 well enough to meet in person. With each e-mail, with each date, I was able to practice flirting and build back my confidence that I was an attractive, desirable woman. Of even greater value, through trial and laughable errors, I pinpointed the unique values and traits that I needed and wanted in a mate.

I found him. The man I prayed for. The man I knew I would marry when his plan for our second date included a finger-sucking dinner of blue crabs in Chinatown, followed by a concert of Civil War ballads at an Irish bar in Greenwich Village. It was a crazy date but perfect for us because it blended the stories we shared about our Southern childhoods into the urban landscape we loved.

It's almost six years to the day of that date, and we're so unabashedly happy and grateful to have found each other that friends from our van pool tease us, "Don't you guys ever have a bad day?" We don't. We're extraordinarily compatible, and we have online dating to thank for this fortuitous match.

WHY DOES ONLINE DATING WORK?

Dating is a numbers game, and online dating has the best odds. For women over 35, when it comes to dating, the smart money is betting on the computer. The numbers tell the tale:

✦ Up to 37 million people visit online dating services every month.

✦ Forty-three percent of online-personals users are ages 35 to 50; on many big sites, the fastest-growing category is 55+.

✦ Men are more likely to sign up for online dating than women are (60 percent versus 40 percent).

Clearly, the Internet is the world's most extraordinary matchmaker. Online dating not only offers more choices than the blind date and blind fate methods, it also provides *better* choices.

Excellent at massaging data, the computer can search and sort for a range of factors such as age, interests, values, and background. This kind of selection wizardry is essential for success. Studies have shown that like attracts like, so people of the same ethnic group, with similar physical traits, for example, or cultural reference points, tend to marry. Anthropologists call it "positive assortive mating."

Positive assortive mating—compatibility, really—is even more of a key relationship factor for Boomers who've reached their "Miller time": the age of relaxation. With the job of raising children mostly over and lots of life under the belt, the single Boomer is in search of a playful partner: someone to love, to have fun with, and certainly not to argue with over differences. As anthropologist Margaret Mead said, "The first relationship is for sex; the second is for children; the third is for companionship."

Online dating can reach across boundaries to find the perfect compatible companion. It could be someone in a different community or state (as was the case with my second husband and me), or it could be someone who lives practically next door. The computer transcends geography, luck, and timing to make the introduction.

Another strength of computer-generated choices: the candidates self-identify as daters. There's no guesswork about motives. Every man online has taken time and effort to post a profile. In doing so he is announcing, "I'm in the market for a relationship. I want to meet someone." It would take years and years to round up the pool of eager daters that is electronically gathered in seconds.

THE COMPUTER OFFERS DATING WITH DIGNITY

For the mature single woman, the thought of heading to a singles' bar to meet someone is about as appealing as entering a wet T-shirt competition in Cancun over spring break. Some things are just better left to youngsters.

Imagine, however, sitting at your desk at home, a glass of chilled white wine at your side. As you browse through the new e-mail prospects who responded to your online profile, you chuckle at some messages, delete a few others, and type flirtatious replies to the keepers.

Welcome to dating with dignity!

Going online takes the sting of rejection out of mate selection. Compare old-time to online dating:

Old-Time	Online
High anxiety	High comfort
Rejection	Preselection
Personally embarrassing	Anonymously impersonal
Must be aggressive to win	Must be active to win
Chosen	Chooser
Random pool of men	Receptive pool of men
Quick, chancy meeting of strangers	Chance to get acquainted before meeting (less "strangerous")

WHAT'S HOLDING YOU BACK?

I'm convinced that online dating offers the best choices with the least bother for women our age. If you're still hesitant to give it a try, I think I know the reasons that may be stopping you. I want to walk you through some briefly here—there's more detail in the chapters to come—because I want you to take advantage of the best way to find a loving partner.

"It's not romantic." Do you think love letters are romantic? E-mails are the new billets-doux. You'd have to go back to the 18th century to find men as willing to write about their inner feelings. What's more, as an online wooer reveals his heart's desires, it's as if he sells himself on love. Perhaps that's why, according to studies, online daters fall in love faster and are quicker to wed than couples who first meet face-to-face.

"It's not safe." Here's some consolation for being older: you're one of the least likely targets for undesirables. Still, I talked to experts on lying and photo fraud, and interviewed the Date Detective. A whole chapter is devoted to protecting you—or, more likely, any woman under 30 that you know—from deceit, harassment, and assault.

"Men my age go for younger women." Not so. The demographic truth is that men marry women within three years of their own age. *Boomers' Guide* will prepare you to take on any competition—younger or your age, online or off. You'll have the strategies and research to succeed. This is the kind of resource I wish I'd had when I started dating again.

"I'm set in my ways. Why bother?" In a survey conducted by *AARP Magazine*, over one-third of the men and women in their 50s admitted they hadn't been hugged or kissed in the six months preceding the survey. You're made for more. In God's wisdom, humans were granted deep capacities to enjoy companionship. We want to socialize, share our thoughts, laugh, and have fun with a partner. We have strong needs for affection and intimacy with a special person. You can distract yourself or divert your most basic needs, but you're not going to outgrow them, and they're not going away. Believe me, it's better to bother, and *Boomers' Guide* will make it easy to find a mate.

On the practical side, a solid relationship is the best investment you can make to ensure a healthier, wealthier, and sexier life for yourself. Consider this:

✦ Married women are less likely to be lonely, depressed, or anxious, according to researchers Linda J. Waite and Maggie Gallagher, authors of *The Case for Marriage*.

✦ Wives are almost 40 percent less likely than unmarried women to say their health is poor.

↑ Two may not live as cheaply as one, but, according to a study published by the National Academy of Sciences, they can live as cheaply as one and a half.

↑ Single women not only earn less than either married or single men, they earn an average of $6,000 less than married women, according to a 2002 salary survey report from CareerBank.com.

↑ Among people nearing retirement, married people's assets are more than twice as high as those of single people.

↑ Married people are about twice as likely as unmarried people to make love two or three times a week.

With your health, wealth, and happiness at stake, can you afford to sit on the relationship sidelines? It pays in every way to find a life partner.

JOIN THE DATE QUAKE

Like me, you're a Boomer. We're used to throwing our demographic weight around. That hasn't changed since we were babies. What's the fastest-growing group in the country? People 50 to 54. Second fastest? Folks 45 to 49. And 16 million Boomers—more than 25 percent of all Boomers—are single. Right behind are 13 million mature, single Gen Xers. It's a veritable third-age date quake!

Boomers' boisterous, never-say-old attitude adds to the party mix. We're not a member of the Silent Generation that quietly retired from the social action at 50. We defined the Youth Culture and, from the sheer power of our numbers, we've forced a vitality extension: Fifty is the new 30; 60, the new 40. With that kind of math, Boomers could be hot-date material for the next half century.

Resurrect your Boomer attitude. Revive your optimism, activism, and sense of fun. March yourself to the computer and change your world. *Boomers' Guide* will be there to help you with every step you take toward happiness.

PART

One

DEFINING COMPATIBILITY

GET READY FOR A RELATIONSHIP

DISCOVER THE RIGHT TYPE
OF MAN FOR YOU

OVERCOME THE ROADBLOCKS
TO SUCCESS

1

ARE YOU RELATIONSHIP-READY?

Before you even think about browsing all those dating sites, find out whether you're psychologically prepared to embark on a new relationship. Take this quick quiz.

1. My past relationships, though painful at times, have taught me to be more caring and accepting.   True False

2. Men are a lot of fun to be with.   True False

3. I'm a lot of fun to be with.   True False

4. An intimate and loving relationship is a top priority for me.   True False

5. I believe I can shape my future.   True False

6. Men are so irresponsible. Frankly, I don't know why I'm bothering to look for one.   True False

7. I'm looking for a man to make me happy.   True False

8. Love is destiny. If a relationship is meant to be, the right man will find me.   True False

9. I can take or leave sex.   True False

10. Shopping and dining at a good restaurant are
two of my favorite activities.   True   False

Scoring: If you answered "true" to questions 1 through 5 and "false" to 6 through 10, you're ripe for love. You've learned a lot from your life experiences. You have a joyful, vibrant, can-do way of thinking, and you're open to sharing with a like-minded, intimate partner. Breeze through this chapter to fine-tune your potential. Did you miss a few answers? You may want to reflect on your feelings about men and rev up your enthusiasm. This chapter will help you feel organized, in control, and headed for a good thing. It's your crash course in relationship-readiness.

WHAT IS READY?

Readiness is all about attitude, about being emotionally prepared to date. Do you match this formula?

R: Recovered from the past, hopeful about the future
E: Engaged in activities that make you fun and interesting to be with
A: Accepting attitude toward men
D: Destined for love because you believe you can shape your destiny
Y: Yearning to connect and communicate with a loving and nurturing partner who respects your values, shares your interests, and wants a close relationship

If this doesn't describe you, let's get you READY.

Recovered from the Past

I've been there. *There*—where you're hurt, sad, angry, disappointed, and, most of all, alone.

I remember exactly when I moved from there to here. At the time, simple, everyday tasks overwhelmed my ability to cope. One of the most frustrating was gathering quarters for the laundry machines in my co-op's basement. I never could get to the bank before it closed, so I spent the week asking for change from cranky store clerks. In one store I braced myself for the usual "I can only give you four quarters," when, instead, a woman smiled and said, "I'll give you all that you need."

I'm sure she was an angel in disguise, because she had the words to comfort me and help me examine my life in a way I never had before. What all *did* I need? What would it take to feel abundantly whole? What did I need to do and know so I would stop repeating the same old mistakes?

The first thing I had to do was clear my heart. I realized I was a scorekeeper—an unfair one at that. Some days, the unarticulated rules for getting along with me revolved around romance. Points were deducted for

A WIDOW GETS READY

"Dating is a very different experience for a widow," says my sister, Becky Cochran, whose husband died unexpectedly eight years ago at age 47. "When you're going through a divorce, some part of you is happy to be out of the marriage. Not me. I miss so much about my marriage to Jim. It's a loss that will never end.

"Friends who urged me to date early on didn't understand that for me moving on meant leaving behind. It's just very hard to find the will to replace someone you adored. My youngest son was the one who gave me the push I needed. I asked him to come with me to a neighborhood wiener roast. He put his hands on my shoulders and turned me to face him. 'Mom,' he said, 'it's time you dated.'"

As she tests the waters of dating, Becky has already found benefits she enjoys: "I'm happy when I'm not the odd place at a dinner party, and I had really missed male company. It took a while, but I'm looking forward to finding the right companion." ⬩

any perceived waning attentiveness and ardor. An imperceptible mood switch later, and the score hedged on household helpfulness. ("If you loved me," according to this game, "you should be able to remember to bring home tall kitchen garbage bags with handles. They were on the list!") I called my mate on everything. I couldn't let anything go. Disappointments accrued like back taxes. They were cumulative and compounded, neither forgotten nor forgiven.

I didn't want to bring this grouchy taskmaster, with her indiscernible playbook and unpardonable scoring system, into a new relationship. I ceased tallying my hurts and examined ways I'd been hurtful myself—inattentive, critical, unresponsive, and self-righteous. As soon as I owned up to my own faults, admitted my own poor performance and responsibility in my choices, actions, and attitude, I felt free of the power of the past. I was open to the new and eager to learn.

Be an angel to yourself. Examine the past, and then release it. Tear up the scorecard and start fresh. If you don't, the legacy will seep out in big and little ways—in unappealing sarcasm, defensiveness, sadness, brittleness, criticism, or control. Let go to make space for positive feelings and behavior. (More below and in chapter 2.)

Engaged in Fun Activities

If you answered "true" to question 10, it's time to branch out. A range of interests and recreational activities (beyond shopping) will add pep to your life. You'll feel energized and more fulfilled. You'll lose the desperate feeling that you need a man to make you happy, because you'll be happier with yourself.

Even if you're already involved in a number of pursuits, consider adding something new. Psychologists say that familiar routines keep us locked into roles and attitudes. Mixing things up can be like a vacation from your old self, a chance to renew and replenish. Activities that excite you give life value, suggests Robert Firestone, Ph.D., in his book *The Fantasy Bond*. According to a survey by the Yankelovich Monitor, 67

SOMETHING FOR THE MIND

Some social scientists say midlife adults should be called "zoomers" instead of Boomers, given the preoccupation with youthfulness and the penchant to play hard. In one study, Boomers say they consider age 79 to be old. As long as there's a zest for living and a desire to grow, the feeling seems to be that time doesn't register.

Over three-quarters of the zippy bunch say they feel the need to get more pleasure out of life, according to Yankelovich, and that means going all out for both physical and intellectual activities. Along with sports like golf, exercise walking, or bowling (see appendix), Boomers pursue challenges that help them learn, explore creative outlets, and find excitement.

If you're thinking of branching out and trying something new, consider learning a different language, craft, or hobby, such as pottery or photography, or how to cook an exotic cuisine. Join a painting class; take up an instrument; find acting or choral groups. You can also just appreciate the arts: bone up on opera, jazz, or the blues; attend museum shows, gallery openings, and art or music festivals. Get outside: take a nature, astronomy, or gardening course; learn how to show dogs or spot birds, whales, or moose. Be a ringside fan: head to golf, fishing, and tennis tournaments; basketball, baseball, and football games; auto races and marathons. Take a tour of historic, cultural, and ethnic sites; check out parks, vineyards, and gardens. Give something back by volunteering at church or the hospital, or for a political candidate. Or be a little wicked and play the slots or Texas hold 'em. When you travel, as Boomers often do, take advantage of excursions and learn-as-you-go opportunities.

Your life can be a continuing adventure. Be one of the zoomers that never gives in to age and atrophy. You'll feel happier with yourself, and you'll come across as a happier person. In the following chapters, you'll also see how a richness of activities adds to your profile, questionnaire, and e-mails. It's an added advantage to describe the details of an interesting life. ↖

percent of Boomers would welcome more novelty and change into their lives.

There's also an ulterior motive. Online daters are attracted to those who are enthusiastic and have a sense of playfulness. The more ways you know how to have fun, the better your chances of meeting someone.

To improve your odds even more, try a sport men enjoy (see "Top 10 Matchmaking Activities" on page 209). I can't emphasize enough the value of companionship. For example, in a survey conducted for the book *Love at Second Sight*, by Nancy W. Collins and Mason Grigsby, 400 single men over age 50 rated "common interests" higher than "attractiveness" as the top desired quality in a partner.

Accepting Attitude toward Men

My first husband, in one of his parting shots, accused me of not liking men. I protested vehemently: "Of course I like men. I've had boyfriends since I was ten years old!"

During my period of self-reflection, however, I realized he had my number. Wanting to be with a man is not the same as liking men.

My background made it easy to be biased. I grew up in a family of five girls, with a sweet, loving mother and a charming, difficult father. As you'd suspect, I had a very typical mindset. I idealized my mother and felt my father—and men in general—were domineering and irresponsible.

When I entered the workplace, I again saturated my life with a feminine focus. For 30 years I worked for women's magazines with almost all female staffs. Every month I helped brainstorm and churn out articles on how to improve or cope with men who were incompetent in emotional and personal matters. The prejudices thickened, although they weren't as obvious to me then as they are in retrospect.

As I battled with myself over that tough question of what all did I need, the first thing I had to acknowledge was that I needed a man. I had a dream job and wonderful children, family, and friends. My life was spiritually rich, physically and intellectually robust. But I needed warmth, affection, and sexual intimacy. I wanted a mate.

Locating my desire was important, but I was still not answering the other big question—did I like men? I wrestled some more and surprised myself with the answer: I liked men, but I was jealous of their power and of their fun.

For example, when my first husband would play golf, I'd stay home with the kids, doing errands or cleaning up. I felt morally superior because I was in my "good girl" role, but I also felt weak. My smugness and envy made me chip away at his pleasure—*nobody's having fun in this house, buster!*

I discovered, as I talked to parents in the workshops I conduct, that I was not alone in my ever-cranky, haughty attitude about domestic duties, which is at the core of so much anger directed at men.

One workshop participant, her husband sheepishly beside her, huffed: "He expects applause if he changes the baby's diaper. One day I confronted him, 'How do you think the diapers, wipes, ointment, and sanitized garbage pail got there—the diaper fairy? I have to think of everything. You barely have a clue.'"

There was a lot of truth in her statement, though I doubt it did much to encourage her husband to offer any help ever again.

When it comes to the home front, women usually do have to think of everything. That's how we're wired. A division of labor and specialization in tasks—sexual dimorphism—began about three million years ago, give or take a millennium. Males picked the outdoorsy, physically challenging, dangerous yet stimulating work. Females stuck closer to home, concentrating on gathering food and caring for children. It was a plan.

Jump ahead to the 1970s, when a majority of mothers became equal partners in the outer world of work. One gender now held down an outside job while still gathering food (albeit at the grocery store), managing the household, and caring for the children. The other gender was not as quick to jump in and share a partner's duties. (According to a 2004 study by the Labor Department, men put in half the time mothers do on child care activities and an hour per day less on housework.) Nor were men who agreed to help a mate always that skillful at it. Even when they wanted to pitch in, some bungled shopping lists, shrank the laundry, or failed to anticipate that children need regular meals, baths, and bedtimes.

"When my wife has to travel, the household routine unravels," one

BEWARE OF BASHING

Do you chuckle when you see commercials that portray men as jerks? Read books with titles like *Why Dogs Are Better Than Men*? Perhaps you commiserate with women friends: Gee, guys are so . . .

a. undependable

b. unfaithful

c. unfathomable

Remember the rules from math class: positive times positive equals positive; positive times negative equals negative. Any bit of negative in the equation overrides the positive. Steer clear of stereotypes that color your attitude. One unsuccessful dater I spoke with, for example, explained her poor luck by saying, "All guys really want is someone to cook and clean for them. That's not my thing." I'm sure the real reason for her lack of a match was that men could sense her dislike.

Men and women are different. Indeed, writes Matt Ridley in *The Red Queen*, "mankind may be the mammal with the greatest division of sexual labor and the greatest division of mental differences between the sexes."

Once you buy into the truth that the dissimilarities are hard-wired, and not personality quirks designed to raise your ire, you can learn to love the nature of the beast. Your female ancestors selected mates for their power, courage, and strong egos. So blame them, not him, if he wants to watch or play sports (aggressive substitutes) rather often and would rather poke needles in his eye than clean the toilet. Let go of what you're not getting—a feminine sidekick. Instead, embrace maleness for its boldness, its love of fun and excitement—characteristics you may do well to borrow for yourself. ➴

such fellow confessed in one of my workshop groups. "The kids start whining and say, 'Aren't you going to make dinner?' Then it dawns on me, 'That's right. They need to be fed.' I have a momentary panic before I check the refrigerator. Sure enough, my wife has prepared something that I just have to stick in the oven."

After talking to thousands of fuming women and confused men, and from my own hard-won experience, I see a way to a truce in the battle of the sexes. Perhaps these tips can help you defuse some of the stored-up resentment that may block you from liking men.

First, get over yourself. It's a marvel that a woman can keep track of and handle so much minutia. Your millions-of-years-old DNA legacy (nature) and decades of nurture (I'll just bet you played with dolls, not trucks) prepared you to be an amazing multitasking wonder. Organizing the kids and planning a weekly menu are easier for your brain to process because of your innate makeup and conditioning. You should be proud of your talent for the domestic—and the skill with which you apply it. It does not make you the superior being, however. So if you—like I once did—think, rather pompously, that tackling the traditional women's work earns special Brownie points for you, while not doing so rates a guy a spot in the lowest ring of hell, you may want to adjust the attitude.

Second, promise never to argue over who cleans the toilet bowl. I sometimes believe most conflicts between the sexes start with this sticking point. It's the front line of modern-day relationship turf battles. There are dozens of products, from little blue bowl cleaners to disposable brushes that make this an easy hands-off task. Trade the scrub work for a promise to change all future flat tires, or come up with another compromise. But don't turn it into an ego-deflating issue. It's not worth the collateral damage.

Next, reduce your rumination. Women spend much more time than men do in pointless thinking, either reviewing the past ("Where did I go wrong?") or worrying about the future ("Will I ever lose weight?"). It's like stepping on the accelerator with the car in park, using a lot of energy but getting nowhere. Rumination also elevates levels of the hormone cortisol, which increases stress.

The brain much prefers to be actively engaged—engrossed in figuring out a crossword puzzle, for example—or quietly contemplative, as when you meditate or chant.

Health and peace of mind improve without all that worthless pondering. Relationships even more so. Because once you get bored with self-blame, remorse, and negative personal projections, your thoughts nat-

PRIMARY RESEARCH ON MEN

Have you been living in a world of women? Would you like to discover the land of men? The best way to explore this different territory is to learn from the natives themselves. Listening to men—as opposed to hearing what girlfriends, your mother, your therapist, or the media have to say about them—helps you to understand the real nuances of their thoughts and feelings, keep up with their deepest concerns and interests, and get their jokes like an insider. Going to the source opens new levels of communication, intimacy, and appreciation.

One of the best places to start hearing true male patter is the *Imus in the Morning* radio show. I have to admit that when I first heard the program, while driving with Walter, I couldn't believe that Don Imus, who seemed pompous, could be so popular with men. Then, as I got used to the banter between Imus and regulars Charles, Bernie, and Sid, I converted to a fan. (I still think Sid's a chauvinistic moron—that's kind of his distinction—but the other guys pound him for it. Bernie literally beat him up once.) What I've come to appreciate from the show, also seen on MSNBC, is how straightforward, loyal (depending on the mood), and funny men can be. If you want to know what guys think, feel, ridicule, and revere, here's your psychological sample. And if you call me a sucking-up weasel, you'll sound just like Imus.

Here's another way to learn about men and keep up with their interests. How much of ESPN Outdoors or Outdoor Life Network (OLN) do you watch? One of our TV sets stays tuned to those channels. Every time I pass

urally turn to . . . him! "Why does he always do that? How come I can't count on him? Why doesn't he make me happier?" And on and on.

He, meanwhile, is sandbagged. "Where did this dissonance come from?" he might wonder. "Honey, have you been ruminating again?" (though he might not use these words).

Self-knowledge is wisdom, but beware as soon as it becomes brooding. Then it's a case of self-flagellation, which is likely to end in beating up on a partner. Stop mulling and move on. Read a juicy novel, play cards, call

through the room, I glimpse an unsuspecting wild turkey being called to its death. (I much prefer the weekend show in which fish get kissed and released.) Still, thanks to ESPN Outdoors and OLN, I'm fairly conversant now in the blood sports. Why, you might be thinking, would I want to talk about hunting and fishing? Because I enjoy understanding the enthusiasms of my second husband, Walter. I like to stay abreast of all his passions, the same way he makes an effort to keep up with mine.

I also tune into sports radio. Mike and the Mad Dog keep me current on the burning controversies of the day, which in my area center around the Mets and the Yankees, the Giants and the Jets; to trade or not to trade; whether to blame the game results on the owner, manager, player(s), or fans. I'm sure if you substituted the name of the teams, the heated discussions on sports radio where you are would be pretty much the same.

If you're really clever, you'll make Comedy Central a favorite on the remote and tape the monologues of Jay Leno, David Letterman, and Conan O'Brien. Humor scores big with the opposite sex. According to research from dating sites eHarmony.com and Match.com, after character, humor is the trait men prefer most.

My point? You're not in the market for a woman friend. Your target is men. Don't get the scoop on your target from sitcoms, reality shows, or other women. Do the primary research so you can find out what tickles a man or ticks him off. At the very least you'll be able to talk turkey.

your best friend. Keep your mind busy so that you don't turn on yourself or him.

A final tip: If someone has something you want, you can be bitter—or you can try to get it for yourself. As I said, I was envious when my first husband played golf while I saddled myself with dutiful drudge work. (I could easily have arranged play dates for the kids and joined him, a strategy he suggested.) When I became single I realized my bitterness wasn't productive or attractive, so I took up the very sport that seemed to be the lightning rod for my jealousy. And it was golf, ironically, that changed my attitude and answered my questions: What do I need? Do I like men?

Out on a beautiful course, making a great shot, I felt strong and free and incredibly happy. I had never experienced such unbridled joy. *So this is their secret*, I thought. *Men aren't stuck in self-denial. They know how to have fun and make it a priority.* On the spot, I gave myself permission to enjoy. I wanted to be a good sport—generous, lighthearted, accepting, noncontrolling, full of fun. And I wanted to be a man's kind of woman, because, finally, I knew how much I liked men.

I was 50 before I figured all this out. I hope you're ahead of me on this score, or perhaps your issues are different. If, however, you find yourself generalizing about men, putting them down, or feeling frustrated because you can't control them, ask yourself the questions. Don't stop until you have acceptable answers.

Destined for Love

A woman who is used to managing her life powerfully and effectively in all other spheres can be wimpy when it comes to intimate relationships. She might be savvy enough to know that she can't wait for the perfect job to magically cross her path. She'll prepare, network, and interview to find the right spot. The same person who's proactive about her career, however, may think she can sit and wait for a special man to drop from the sky and onto her doorstep. She doesn't lift a finger to influence her personal future. Could that be you?

Don't let romantic notions get in the way of finding real romance. Keep sentiment from coloring how you view life. It has a way of making a person either wistfully wishy-washy or harshly jaded. Being realistic and optimizing your options will net you a relationship far faster than merely fantasizing about one will. Even Cinderella, the quintessential dreamy heroine, snapped to attention and worked with her fairy godmother to snag Prince Charming. The computer could be your magic wand, if you can conjure up the will to try it.

Fear may also be holding you back: "I don't know how to date. What if I fail?" Once you've read *Boomers' Guide*, you'll have gained confidence, and each time you go out you'll learn something new, not just about dating, but about yourself: how men react to you and what you want in a relationship. You'll discover that there are no failed dates, but you can fail yourself by not trying at all. Psychologists say that it's the things you don't do that creates the most regret.

Sometimes Boomers get engulfed in the fatigue factor—the "why bothers." These examples may ring a bell: "I'm sick of this job, but who'd hire someone my age?" "I've always wanted to travel, but never got around to it." Or the ultimate give-up-without-trying: "I just can't seem to find the right man."

When I was slogging through one of those low-energy, enervating spells, my friend Kate rescued me. She was awesome.

"I can't believe I'm listening to this," she stormed. "After all you've been through, all you've learned and accomplished, you're going to sit back and give up. I never thought you'd let yourself be defined by failure!"

It was a very effective wake-up call. Here's yours: You have too much experience to draw upon, too much potential to fulfill, to cop out just when life is getting really sweet and every day of it counts. Don't let fantasies, fears, or fatigue hold you back from the prospect of happiness. Don't make decisions on the basis of silly notions, insecurity, or inertia. You have the good sense, the courage, and the strength to shape your own love destiny.

Yearning to Connect

When I took up golf, it gave me a chance to play and talk with male friends. I figured they would have the best advice about what men wanted, and I was open to learning from them.

As I said, my first lesson was that a man makes his happiness a priority. Lesson number two was that a guy is just as concerned about the contentment of the woman in his life. He's not truly happy unless she's happy. He would like her to have as much fun as he has—if only she would. Her fulfillment and the quality of their companionship are core issues.

Then there's sex.

My second husband, Walter, came home laughing one day and told me this story. A friend from college had called him out of the blue. "Here's this guy, a hotshot lawyer, and I hadn't heard from him in twenty-five years. The first words out of his mouth were, 'Walter, are you getting any?'"

Before I liked men, that story would have annoyed me. Now it confirms for me the wonderment of men's passion. Sex is *the* headline story of their day, every day. Walter's pal was just very frank about it.

Man's "relentless desire for women," as Nancy Friday describes it in her book *Men in Love*, is their greatest compliment and their strongest need.

The writer Matt Ridley suggests that the central theme of our evolution has been sexual. In his book, *The Red Queen*, he writes: "Why sex? Surely there are features of human nature other than this one overexposed and troublesome procreative pastime. True enough, but reproduction is the sole goal for which human beings are designed; everything else is a means to that end. Human beings inherit tendencies to survive, to eat, to think, to speak, and so on. But above all they inherit a tendency to reproduce."

I found out what men hope for: a woman who is happy with herself and happy to be with him; a woman who, according to Dr. Firestone, "has not given up her sexuality and emotional involvement with men."

Do you yearn for a loving partner whose greatest satisfaction is your satisfaction? Someone who wants to be joyful with you, careful of your feelings, nurturing of your dreams, fulfilling of your passions? Don't say you're too old, too resigned, or too wounded to bother. You were wired for love the moment you were born. It's in your genetic makeup, passed down to you from millions of years ago, a longing that never leaves. Make it happen for yourself. Opt for a life of fun, excitement, and intimacy with a partner. Get READY for the best that's yet to be.

2

WHOM ARE YOU LOOKING FOR?

It's likely that you know what you don't want—someone like your former husband or boyfriend. Getting to the heart of what you do want, however, is not so simple. You may not have looked for a mate in decades, and your choices now will differ in many ways from the ones you made in your 20s or 30s. Companionship, for example, may be more important to you at this age than charm, or sincerity may trump the coolness that was so essential at 16.

The exercises in this chapter are thoughtful probes designed to update your criteria, spotlight your own relationship skills, and pinpoint weaknesses. After completing and reflecting on the exercises, you will have a clearer idea about what you want in a mate and feel more confident about your potential as a partner. You're really going to enjoy learning about yourself and your desires—and you'll be surprised. Your answers will also be used in upcoming chapters to build a relationship résumé and to find the person who meets your needs now. These could very well be the most productive exercises of your life.

EXERCISE NO 1:
Your Love Stories

Here's the advantage you have over younger women and your younger self: experience. Life has taught you a great deal, even if you haven't been paying close attention. This exercise will help your recall.

Write down the relationship experiences that stand out in your mind. Which ones made you feel happy, desirable, and content? Which ones made you feel anxious and angry, lonely, or inadequate? You can start with childhood: *I met my first boyfriend in fourth grade. We both liked science class, baseball, and scary movies.* You can recount fleeting events: *John asked me to the prom. We stayed out until dawn talking about our futures.* You can break a relationship into segments: *Our honeymoon was intensely passionate. By our fifth anniversary, we had so little in common, there was nothing to talk about.* Try to come up with about 20 examples.

1. _____

2. _____

3. _____

4. _____

5. _____

6. _____

7. _____

8. _____

9. _____

10. _____

11. _____

12. _____

13. _____

14. _____

15. _____

16. _____

17. _____

18. _____

19. _____

20. _____

Circle the best 10 of these examples, the ones you recall most fondly. Rank them according to the ones that make you smile the most. Then answer the following questions about your top selections:

Love Story No. 1:

What did you contribute to the relationship?

_____

_____

_____

What was your best quality?

_____

_____

_____

What did you enjoy most?

_____

_____

_____

What did he contribute?

_____

_____

_____

What did you like best about him?

_____

_____

_____

Is there anything you would have done differently?

_____

_____

_____

Love Story No. 2:

What did you contribute to the relationship?

_____

_____

_____

What was your best quality?

_____

_____

_____

What did you enjoy most?

_____

_____

_____

What did he contribute?

_____

_____

_____

What did you like best about him?

_____

_____

_____

Is there anything you would have done differently?

_____

_____

_____

Love Story No. 3:

What did you contribute to the relationship?

_____

_____

_____

What was your best quality?

_____

_____

_____

What did you enjoy most?

_____

_____

_____

What did he contribute?

_____

_____

_____

What did you like best about him?

_____

_____

_____

Is there anything you would have done differently?

_____

_____

_____

Love Story No. 4:

What did you contribute to the relationship?

_____

_____

_____

What was your best quality?

_____

_____

_____

What did you enjoy most?

_____

_____

_____

What did he contribute?

_____

_____

_____

What did you like best about him?

_____

_____

_____

Is there anything you would have done differently?

_____

_____

_____

Love Story No. 5:

What did you contribute to the relationship?

_____

_____

_____

What was your best quality?

_____

_____

_____

What did you enjoy most?

_____

_____

_____

What did he contribute?

_____

_____

_____

What did you like best about him?

_____

_____

_____

Is there anything you would have done differently?

_____

_____

_____

Love Story No. 6:

What did you contribute to the relationship?

_____

_____

_____

What was your best quality?

_____

_____

_____

What did you enjoy most?

_____

_____

_____

What did he contribute?

_____

_____

_____

What did you like best about him?

_____

_____

_____

Is there anything you would have done differently?

_____

_____

_____

Love Story No. 7:

What did you contribute to the relationship?

_____

_____

_____

What was your best quality?

_____

_____

_____

What did you enjoy most?

_____

_____

_____

What did he contribute?

_____

_____

_____

What did you like best about him?

_____

_____

_____

Is there anything you would have done differently?

_____

_____

_____

Love Story No. 8:

What did you contribute to the relationship?

_____

_____

_____

What was your best quality?

_____

_____

_____

What did you enjoy most?

_____

_____

_____

What did he contribute?

_____

_____

_____

What did you like best about him?

_____

_____

_____

Is there anything you would have done differently?

_____

_____

_____

Love Story No. 9:

What did you contribute to the relationship?

_____

_____

_____

What was your best quality?

_____

_____

_____

What did you enjoy most?

_____

_____

_____

What did he contribute?

_____

_____

_____

What did you like best about him?

_____

_____

_____

Is there anything you would have done differently?

_____

_____

_____

Love Story No. 10:

What did you contribute to the relationship?

_____

_____

_____

What was your best quality?

_____

_____

_____

What did you enjoy most?

_____

_____

_____

What did he contribute?

_____

_____

_____

What did you like best about him?

_____

_____

_____

Is there anything you would have done differently?

_____

_____

_____

EXERCISE NO. 2:
Building Your Relationship Résumé

Review your answers to exercise 1. What are you discovering about yourself? What do you contribute to relationships? What are your best qualities? Here's your tally sheet. Mark each trait that you demonstrated in each love story. Be sure to include all 10 stories.

Love story	1	2	3	4	5	6	7	8	9	10	Total
Accepting											
Adventurous											
Affectionate											
Cheerful											
Compassionate											
Considerate											
Creative											
Down-to-earth											
Easygoing											
Empathetic											
Energetic											
Even-tempered											
Friendly											
Funny											
Fun to be with											
Good listener											
Good talker											

Love story	1	2	3	4	5	6	7	8	9	10	Total
Honest											
Intelligent											
Interesting to be with											
Kind											
Outgoing											
Personable											
Polite											
Positive attitude											
Quiet											
Reliable											
Respectable											
Romantic											
Self-confident											
Sensitive											
Sensual											
Sexually passionate											
Sincere											
Spiritual											
Supportive											
Talented											
Trustworthy											
Other:											

Okay, so how did you do? Which qualities earned the most points? These are your natural strengths—the areas in which you're charming and appealing. It's good to remember how much you have to give. Save this list for chapter 4 to help create your Internet profile. But also examine your low scores. Are there things you'd like to improve?

EXERCISE NO. 3:
Man Sorting

Internet dating is the fastest, most efficient way to gather a pool of qualified candidates. It could take you a lifetime to do the investigation that the computer comes up with in seconds. To put that technology to work for you, begin with good data. Eliminate all the losing propositions right from the start.

Review your 10 best love stories. You now have self-knowledge about your strengths and weaknesses, but it's time to evaluate the men in your life so far. What were their best qualities? How did they contribute to your relationships? Mark each trait for each guy in your 10 best love stories. Be sure to include all 10 stories.

Love story	1	2	3	4	5	6	7	8	9	10	Total
Accepting											
Adventurous											
Affectionate											
Cheerful											
Compassionate											
Considerate											
Creative											
Down-to-earth											
Easygoing											
Empathetic											
Energetic											
Even-tempered											
Friendly											
Funny											
Fun to be with											
Good listener											

Love story	1	2	3	4	5	6	7	8	9	10	Total
Good talker											
Honest											
Intelligent											
Interesting to be with											
Kind											
Outgoing											
Personable											
Polite											
Positive attitude											
Quiet											
Reliable											
Respectable											
Romantic											
Self-confident											
Sensitive											
Sensual											
Sexually passionate											
Sincere											
Spiritual											
Supportive											
Talented											
Trustworthy											
Other:											

What qualities earned the most points? What personality types or characteristics are you drawn to? Transfer the top 10 scores of man-sorting traits to the Must List in exercise 7 on page 46.

EXERCISE NO. 4:
Relationship Mapping

Return to your original list of 20 love stories and then think about the 10 relationship experiences you didn't circle. To sort out your thoughts, quickly write down the reasons. Here's a template you might want to use:

I felt _____ (unhappy, anxious, angry, bored, lonely, etc.) with _____ because he was _____ (inconsiderate, unmotivated, a terrible listener, etc.).

Do you see any common themes in your less successful stories?

_____

_____

_____

_____

Are there characteristics or personality types that spell real trouble for you?

_____

_____

_____

_____

What have you learned from these mistakes?

_____

_____

_____

_____

EXERCISE NO. 5:
Background Basics

Studies show that we are drawn to people like ourselves. The most successful relationships are between individuals from the same ethnic group with similar socioeconomic backgrounds, religious values, and levels of education. There are always wonderful exceptions, but the research makes a powerful case for birds of a feather flying off together. Write your preferences for these key factors (race, ethnicity, socioeconomic background, religion, education) below. Other basics might include your strong preferences for a specific geographic area, age range, children not living at home, no smoking, no alcohol or drug addiction, or no pets. Write these down, too. Then add a total of 10 Background Basics to your Must List in exercise 7 on page 46.

EXERCISE NO. 6:
10 Desires

In exercises 1 through 4, you rediscovered the qualities that make you happy or unhappy in a partner. Exercise 5 covered fundamental issues. But there are other factors to consider: other personality traits, shared habits, parallel interests, leisure activities—and, naturally, physical appeal. Here's where you really have to be discerning. You're welcome to add more traits to this list. But drill it down to your 10 Desires. This will really make you think.

Physical:
__ Clothing
__ Eye color
__ Facial hair
__ Good health
__ Hair
__ Handsomeness
__ Height
__ Neatness
__ Physique
__ Sexually functional
__ Works out regularly

Entertainment:
__ Concerts
__ Dancing
__ Hobbies
__ Movies
__ Museums
__ Music
__ TV
__ Other: _____

_____

Intellectual pursuits:

___ The arts

___ Current events and politics

___ History

___ Nature studies

___ Reading

___ Science/technology

___ Other: _____

Leisure:

___ I prefer to be active (bowling, golf, hiking, tennis, etc.).

___ I prefer quiet endeavors (bingo, bridge, crafts, etc.).

___ I like to travel.

___ I like to stay close to home.

Living habits (circle preferences):

Early riser/Late riser

Healthy eater/Whatever

Neat and orderly home/Comfortably livable

Organized/Relaxed

Productive and goal-oriented/Free-spirited

Punctual/Not a clock-watcher

Social (circle preferences):

Like to socialize, party/Avoid crowds and big events

Prestige or pride important/Like a down-home type

Upscale lifestyle/Simple lifestyle

Write down your top 10 Desires on the Must List in exercise 7 on page 46. Was it difficult to get down to 10? The harder the choices, the clearer you'll be about your priorities. Will you trade facial hair for travel, a good dresser for a good dancer? There's a strong chance you can get all that you want—the Internet helps you optimize your options. Meanwhile, you'll know the core values of your heart and mind. This may keep you from being too picky, ruling out solid guys on trivial points before giving them a real chance to shine. And it can protect you from mistakes by holding you to your own true standards.

EXERCISE NO. 7:
Must List (or, 30 Ways to Choose a Lover)

What is your framework for happiness? Your Must List now includes what you've learned from your past; the top 10 traits from your Man Sorting worksheet; the 10 Background Basics that set up the foundation for a relationship; and your 10 Desires. Spend time analyzing your Must List and *hold on to it.* You'll need it in every phase of finding a relationship, right down to the final commitment.

Top 10 Man–Sorting Traits (from exercise 3):

1. _____
2. _____
3. _____
4. _____
5. _____
6. _____
7. _____
8. _____
9. _____
10. _____

10 Background Basics (from exercise 5):

11. _____
12. _____
13. _____
14. _____

15. _____

16. _____

17. _____

18. _____

19. _____

20. _____

10 Desires (from exercise 6):

21. _____

22. _____

23. _____

24. _____

25. _____

26. _____

27. _____

28. _____

29. _____

30. _____

EXERCISE NO. 8:
Vision Quest

Make a conscious wish and send it out to the cosmos to be answered. Use your Must List to create a portrait of the man you're looking for. Your vision will get the powers of the universe working for you, and, more practically, it will be helpful in developing your profile and questionnaire, which we'll tackle in chapters 4 and 5.

I'm seeking a man who is . . .

_____

_____

_____

. . . who likes to . . .

_____

_____

_____

The object of these eight exercises is to get stronger and leaner. As you reflected on all the positives in your past love life, you pumped up your self-assurance and latent romantic powers. If you worked off some of the old negative baggage, you're lighter and freer to move on to better times and better people. The choices you made here will direct you there. But let's be absolutely sure there are no other barriers in your way.

RESOURCES

Match.com offers two free online tests—on personality and physical attraction—to evaluate your type of guy.

PerfectMatch.com lets you examine personality factors and similar and complementary traits for free.

The Perfect Partner Test—free on iVillage.com—promises to help you discover your relationship style and what kind of person is the best love match for you today. ↖

3

ROADBLOCKS
TO SUCCESS

Many women become online dating dropouts before giving it a chance to work. They may try a few free searches but never post a profile to make contact with a potential match. They may also stop short when it comes to adding a photo or completing the application. Often the lack of effort is a convenient excuse. The real roadblock is more complex. In my interviews, I found 10 barriers. Is one of these stopping you?

ROADBLOCK NO. 1:
Shyness

Jean, a divorced teacher in her late 40s, is kind, sensitive, and intelligent—the very qualities any sensible man would want in a woman. But Jean is also shy and modest. She looked at profiles posted by young, sexually assertive women and couldn't imagine describing herself that way.

Her daughter, Courtney, and I teamed up to get Jean online. We reassured her that she could be her sweet, quiet self and find plenty of men who would appreciate her. Courtney and I helped Jean find the words that painted a flattering yet truthful picture of her. Here's what she came up with:

ShyOne

READY FOR A SWEET-HEARTED WOMAN?

"I am very warm and caring, as well as smart and interesting. I'm a low-maintenance type who prefers plain to fancy, walking to jogging, mysteries to reality shows. I really don't like to talk about myself much. I'd rather listen to what you have to say. Once I get to know you, though, you'll enjoy our thoughtful, funny conversations."

Jean's profile caught the attention of a real honey of a guy, an affectionate, affable, 51-year-old widower named Glenn. Their first date was an early-bird stroll sponsored by a local mall. "I would never have introduced myself if we had happened by chance to meet at the mall," Jean says, "and I probably would have brushed him off if he had tried to talk to me. But we had introduced ourselves already by computer, and I was very comfortable being with him. I wasn't shy at all."

Going online levels the dating playing field for introverts like Jean; she started with a pool of candidates who preferred the quiet type. Going online also offers a chance to get to know someone without the artificial pressure of a bar scene, party, or blind date. E-mails break the ice before meeting, which sets the stage for conversations that are much richer and more natural than "Come here often?"

ROADBLOCK NO. 2:
Waiting for Personal Improvement

"I want to get a face-lift first."

"I plan to get my teeth whitened."

"I need to lose 25 pounds."

Those are some of the excuses I've heard women give for postponing online dating. But I don't believe in waiting until everything about you is perfect. I'll tell you why.

When my first husband and I split up, I looked the absolute worst of my life. The anxiety of the divorce caused me to drop down to a stick figure of 89 pounds. Medicine I was using caused my skin to break out in red, scaling acne. Then a Fifth Avenue hairdresser had a creative vision of me as Winona Ryder. Just when I could have used some hair to hide behind, my face was exposed by the pixie cut from hell. Actually, *cut* isn't the right word; it was more like a shearing. Let me also mention that I was wearing braces with rubber bands to correct my overbite.

There was *nothing* going for me—no body, no cute face or hair. I couldn't even smile because the braces chafed when I did. And yet I met someone, a wonderful person that I dated for a while and then corresponded with for two years.

I'm so glad I had that experience with Rick. While I was getting it together in the looks department, he showed me that common values, mutual interests, and respect were what counted. He also helped me polish my rusty dating skills.

It took a year to pick up some pounds, clear the skin, grow the hair, and lose the braces. If I had hibernated until I felt perfectly presentable, I would not have begun to discover what I needed from a relationship. Waiting would have made me older but not wiser.

I'm all in favor of self-improvement, but your social life can move forward online while the metamorphosis takes place.

ROADBLOCK NO. 3:
What if someone I know sees the ad?

After seven years of being single, Chris, a 45-year-old banker, wanted to go online but hesitated because she felt vulnerable. "I feel safer just staying at home," she told me. "I work in a man's world, and if a client saw my ad, I think I'd be mortified."

"You know, you don't have to post something that looks like an escort-service ad," I replied. "And what would it mean if a client did see your profile? It would mean that he's probably an online dater like you! You'd have something in common—you both think it's smart and modern to optimize your options, and so much more dignified than going to a bar. Besides, more than 15 million people over age 30 try online dating, so it's not as if you're by yourself in this. Wanting a loving relationship and going for it is a very human, very sane thing to do. What's oddball is for a beautiful woman like you to live without companionship, fun, and passion."

Since Chris was still cautious, I suggested that she visit AARPmagazine.org. The site offers a free, interactive Personal Ad Maker that's fast and straightforward (see chapter 4). Chris could compose a profile that kept personal information to a minimum so that there was nothing to embarrass her. I pointed out that she could be more revealing when she reached the e-mail stages of dating.

Finally, I questioned the strategy she was comfortable with: "In seven years, has even one eligible man miraculously dropped by your house to ask you out?"

Chris agreed to post.

ROADBLOCK NO. 4:
It's Not Romantic

Chris is not the only woman out there who wants love to stop by and ring her doorbell. We all hope for those effortless encounters. We're thrilled by stories of the strangers who sit together on a train and feel an instant connection, or the former sweethearts who see each other again at their high school reunion and decide to marry. I know these kind of romantic fantasies can come true because both examples happened to me.

I also know that being practical and helping Cupid out a little can be a better route to romance.

The way I met my second husband, Walter, wasn't easy or effortless. The quest began at a brunch for executive women when I heard two colleagues my age talking about online dating. Their experiences seemed so positive that I thought this might just be the answer to my prayers. But, as is often the case with answered prayers, I didn't get what I thought I wanted the way I wanted to nor when I wanted it.

I thought I wanted a sweet, average guy. I wound up with someone who far exceeded my expectations—the smartest, funniest, most interesting person I've ever known.

The way I envisioned meeting him was by pushing a key and there he'd be: my cyber-darling. I didn't realize at first how important it was to search seriously. It wasn't until I screened thousands of men on dating sites and corresponded with more than a hundred that I became truly discerning. The process was my schooling in emotional maturity.

Frankly, I needed to evolve about men. At 18, I fell in love willy-nilly with my first husband because he was sweet and tall and had the most gorgeous hazel eyes. When we reconnected at a reunion 10 years later, he was still a nice, tall guy with those incredible hazel eyes—so I married him. After our split, my year of cyber-courtship helped me see past my physical type. I became much more attracted to profiles that exemplified companionable qualities such as warm personality, interests, and values. By the time I linked to Walter I was a grown-up with grown-up criteria. The fact that he was tall with astonishing blue eyes was just icing on the cake.

Maybe mine isn't an old-fashioned love story. Yet it's been almost six years since Walter and I met, and every day of our life together is romantic. We can't kiss each other, hug each other, and thank our lucky stars enough. We use so many terms of endearment that a caddy once thought my name was "Honey." We're extraordinarily compatible and humbly grateful for the divine and electronic intervention that connected us.

Every online couple I know considers their story a modern romance. For example, instead of reciting a poem at her wedding two years ago, 51-year-old Stephanie Fischer read her husband Jim's first e-mail to her. "This," she said, "is why I'm marrying this man."

Isn't *that* romantic?

ROADBLOCK NO. 5:
Does It Work?

After her divorce, 55-year-old Susan realized a lifelong dream of moving from suburban Illinois to metropolitan New York. She loved the city and her new job as an editor, but she missed the robust social life she had enjoyed back home. Days would go by with no one to talk to.

When I met Susan at church, I thought she'd be a perfect candidate for online dating. She felt she was too busy with her career to invest time on a long shot. "Besides," she said, "there'll be no men in my age group."

I got her business card and e-mailed her some stats, such as close to 40 million people visit online dating sites every month; 60 percent of them are men; more than 40 percent of all visitors are over age 30.

The best thing about this vast group is that it is comprised of people who self-identify as daters. In fact, they've taken the time and trouble to announce that they want to meet someone. The computer then takes this qualified pool of cooperative prospects and starts sorting: by age, geography, interests, pets or no pets, smoking or nonsmoking, on and on. By the time the electronic sorting is over, the millions may be down to hundreds or dozens. Or just one—the right one, the only one you need.

Match.com, the largest online dating site, had 974,000 paying subscribers in 2004, along with millions of browsers (who can post profiles but not make contact). In 2003, the site calculated, based on resignation survey data, that 200,000 subscribers had found the person they were looking for. The search time was less than six months. That's an incredible success rate when you consider how hard it is to find the right person the old-fashioned way: Six percent of Boomers have yet to marry, and half of all Americans who do marry make a mistake that ends in divorce.

I suspect that the Match.com numbers are only the tip of the iceberg. They reflect those who *reported* their good luck. I bet that most subscribers are like me. As soon as I met my husband-to-be, my online dating days were over, and I never followed up with the dating sites. I simply let my subscriptions expire.

When Susan decided to give it a try, she found "many, many more men in my age group than I suspected. I guess I thought of online dating as a fringe activity. I had no idea how popular it was. I actually got responses within an hour."

ROADBLOCK NO. 6:
I'm Set in My Ways

Mary Ann, a 60-year-old saleswoman, with cheerful blue eyes and steel gray hair, had been on her own for over a decade. As she regained her strength and self-esteem post-divorce, she created a lively, independent life for herself. She bought a townhouse in the greater San Francisco Bay area and decorated it slowly and carefully with shabby chic finds from yard sales and flea markets. She became so adept at refinishing forsaken treasures that an antiques dealer offered her a boutique within his store.

She was busy with her job and her decorating sideline but still found time to sing torch songs with a jazz trio twice a month. She also loved babysitting for her four-year-old grandson, Chase. She never tired of helping him build elaborate castles out of blocks. She couldn't wait for him to sit in her lap while she read his favorite Curious George stories. They were so silly, and the two of them laughed together, even though they'd probably read the tales a hundred times or more. She was surprised that at this age she had such patience for play, much more than when she was a young mother herself.

Whenever Mary Ann went through a lonesome spell that her full schedule and a hug from Chase couldn't assuage, she bought another cat. She was up to six, and she admitted that felines had taken over the house.

"They haven't only taken over the house," I suggested to her, as I brushed hair off the couch so I could sit down. "They've taken over your life. A kitty cat is not a substitute for a guy. Plus, do you think a fellow is going to put up with this fur ball palace? You're erecting barriers to a relationship. Do you know that?"

Mary Ann argued that she wasn't sure she wanted a man.

"I like my freedom," she said. "I can buy what I want and do what I want when I want to. I enjoy having everything just the way I like it. I wouldn't want to move a single picture or deal with someone's ugly furniture. And what about Chase or my singing? What if someone objected to my spending time doing the things I love?"

She went on to catalog more advantages of being unattached. "I rarely have to shave my legs—I just wear pants until I disgust myself! I don't have to dye my hair to look younger, either."

"You seem to have a hang-up about hair," I interjected.

"The point is," she continued, "I don't want to change. Take it or leave it."

We spent the rest of the afternoon sharing a chilled bottle of chardonnay and deconstructing her single fortress. A few late-night calls over the years (a stop-gap measure to defer the purchase of a new cat) had led me to believe that she was lonely beneath the frenetic activity. I asked her, between sneezes from all the cats, what she missed about her former marriage, and the floodgates opened.

She missed little things, like not having anyone to scratch the hard to reach spot between her shoulder blades, or bring her an aspirin and water if she had a headache.

And she missed big things. She was unaccountable to anyone—a free pass to indulge her every whim—but that, it turned out, was a double-edged sword. No one knew (or cared) about what she did every day. Her son and daughter were focused on their families, as they should be and as she wanted them to be. Friends were supportive in spurts, but that consistent wellspring of concern that a partner offers daily was absent.

"If it weren't for talking to my cats," she confided, "I'd be mute most evenings. I live in a world of silence."

"So on the positive side," I said, "your single state offers the benefit of not having to rearrange the furniture or put up with a coffee table decoupaged in imported beer labels. You can also keep hair, yours and the cats', the way you like it.

"For argument's sake, let's just suppose that there's a man in this general vicinity who might take an interest in a silver-haired, sexy-voiced singer with superb taste. Let's go out on a limb and say he also likes to visit flea markets. Maybe he'd look forward to spending time with a charming little boy like Chase. Could be he even has grandkids himself and knows how special they are. Mr. X, as we'll call him, is an animal lover, too, though perhaps not to your extent. How does this sound so far?"

"I'm listening," she said.

"So Mr. X—a great conversationalist and back scratcher, by the way—is available and interested. Do you think you could compromise on a few points, perhaps shave on at least a semi-annual basis and maybe downsize a few cats, to get him?"

"Yes!" she answered.

"See," I clinked her wineglass. "You're not inflexible after all."

Like Mary Ann, many women embrace independence so wholeheartedly that they box themselves into an uncompromising corner. The trouble with staying in the corner is that it doesn't offer a vista or room to expand. It's stifling after awhile and, of course, it gets lonely there.

If Mary Ann had given some thought to how patient she was with her grandson, she may have realized that she really wasn't that set in her ways. Her years of life experience had taught her when compromise was rewarding and when it meant giving up a vital part of one's self. Bending somewhat didn't mean she had to break her spirit.

We worked on her profile.

Silver-Haired Songstress

"I'm a successful, independent, 60-year-old professional with an engaging personality and a lot of vitality. I love the outdoors, animals (especially cats), and browsing through flea markets. Water aerobics and romping with my grandson keep me fairly fit. I sing with a band for fun. Let's get to know each other, and I'll sing a special song just for you."

Postscript: Mary Ann posted on three sites. After about a year of online dating, she met a rancher and wine grower from Santa Maria, California. He has six grandkids, and a pickup truck to help her with the flea market shopping. If they decide to marry—and they may if Mary Ann can work out her job situation—the cats are moving to the barn and his ghastly furniture is headed to the basement.

ROADBLOCK NO. 7:
I've Been Burned Before

I sat next to Candy at a luncheon. When the conversation worked its way around to online dating, she stopped me cold. "I tried it two years ago," she said. "I corresponded with a guy for weeks. When we met, he was nothing like I expected. I'll never waste my time again."

Before we turned our attention to that day's speaker, I found out that Candy was still not in a serious relationship. She was waiting, I guess, for the love lottery to surprise her with a winning ticket.

No one wants to waste time, feel duped, or get hurt, and the advice throughout *Boomers' Guide* will minimize those risks. But one bad episode, or even several, is not a reason to write off a method that's proven to work so well for so many daters.

What in life works perfectly the first time you try it? The other day I expertly parallel parked the car. No one was there to applaud. But I was proud that the person who at sixteen was mortified at failing a driving test because of this mechanical maneuver now scooted into a spot with ease. There are countless examples that I could share about not getting something right the first time. I'm glad I don't give up easily. If I did, I never would have survived putting myself through college, or my first winter in New York, or many of my ultimately most rewarding experiences. Perseverance also paid off when I raked through a mountain of e-mails and a spate of dreadful dates until I hit pay dirt—Walter.

The old adage—once burned, twice shy—doesn't mean stop and sur-render. I interpret it as a caution to be thoughtful and learn something for next time. Stay in the game, and go get him.

ROADBLOCK NO. 8:
I'm Not Interested in Sex

If you watch television, you may believe that people our age are invet-erate sex fiends. Every other ad seems to promote a drug such as Viagra. The stars of the ads are mature men, with devilish smiles on their lips, and beside them are midlife women with telltale looks of contentment on their faces. We look like a pretty hot bunch, and some of us are.

However, an estimated 25 percent of premenopausal women, and one in three menopausal women, have low sex drives, according to findings reported by the American Society for Reproductive Medicine. Indeed, a low sex drive is the most common sexual complaint made by women.

Beverly, a 63-year-old systems analyst, was never crazy about the sex-ual side of her marriage. When her husband died, she was not unhappy that that particular wifely duty was at an end. "Well, that's that," she said, stowing away any latent desire.

After a year or so, her kids urged her to get out more. So once a month she donned a red hat and purple pants suit to go out with the ladies. "We meet to eat" was their motto, and lunch sometimes spilled over into the Happy Hour. She had a blast, until a Cosmo or two pulled the topic of conversation around to sex. She didn't know what to say. She'd never been horny like loud-mouthed Regina. (Well, maybe a lit-tle, but she wouldn't broadcast that fact to a group of ten women.) Sex was not something she was good at or wanted to do or wanted to talk about. She was squarely in the thirty-three percent of women with hypoactive sexual desire disorder, as doctors call it. Frigid, is how she labeled it for herself.

There were, however, some things she did miss. She and her husband had collected wine. She still kept the small cellar stocked with bottles of pinot noir, sauvignon blanc, and shiraz. It would be nice to share a good wine again with a man. She wanted to dance, too. She longed for a partner to take her out on the floor, spin her around, and collect her safely in his arms. Sunset walks. Listening to music together. It wasn't men she disliked—they were even better company than the Red Hats. It was the S factor.

Chapter 11 covers a number of ways to revive the libido. But if you, like Beverly, are celibate by choice and determined to stick to your guns, there's good news for you, too. Despite the multimillion dollar ad campaigns, not every man over 45 is popping Viagra like vitamins. Many have opted to put their prowess out to pasture. And it doesn't make them any less loving and romantic.

Sites for seniors (see chapter 6) are especially helpful in selecting potential matches that are not sexually active. No sex does not equal no dates.

ROADBLOCK NO. 9:
I Can't Get My Act Together

Many women want a more robust dating life, but they have trouble setting priorities, getting organized, and moving the ball forward. Let's take these on, one by one.

Your happiness and well-being should always be a chief—if not *the* chief—goal. But maybe you haven't set goals for yourself in a long time. It's fairly common in midlife to drift along until a crisis of some kind demands attention and renewed awareness. Why wait for a shake-up to discover or rediscover your hopes and aspirations? Do a self-review and—this is very important—write down your priorities in order. Save them. Think about them consciously, then put them under your pillow and sleep on them. These are not the same as your promises to yourself to file your recipes or rearrange the linen closet. They deserve concentrated thought.

Make a plan to transform thought into action. Break your goal down into small steps ("Write a headline for my profile," for example) and focus on completing one step a day, or week. Be sure to carry out the step at your peak time of day. Don't put it off while you read your e-mails or listen to phone messages, the way many of us start off the morning. You'll get distracted and move on to other tasks. Put first things first on your agenda.

Chances are, once you take that itty-bitty step, the momentum of doing something positive will ignite your enthusiasm. You may have the entire profile written and posted in no time.

I remember a famous cartoon in which a woman slaps her forehead and the words in the balloon say something like, "Oh, no, I forgot to have children!" I can see how busyness, lethargy, and disorganization can lead to another cartoon: "Oh, no, I forgot to have a love life." Only it's not funny.

ROADBLOCK NO. 10:
I'm Bad with Computers

So am I—really bad. But I had to learn to make peace with a laptop for business as well as social reasons. (It also helps, I confess, to have in-house tech support. Another clever reason to find a mate.)

Libraries and community centers offer excellent—often free—classes on computers. Enrolling in one may be that first step (see above) you need to take. Virtually any child aged five or older can also explain the basics. When it comes to tricky things, like inserting a photo in your ad, most sites have easy, step-by-step instructions, or will do the tough part for you (see chapter 4).

My husband's 86-year-old Aunt Laverne keeps the entire Kirkland clan connected through her e-mails. Age is not an excuse for computer cowardice anymore.

↑

You've now completed Part One. You know yourself a little better, and what you want in a mate, and you've discovered roadblocks that may stand in your way. Next, we get to work on the practical business of developing your dating tools. They'll help you feel confident making a match, even if you're as shy as Jean or as skeptical as Susan.

DEVELOPING YOUR ONLINE DATING TOOLS

CREATE A PROFILE AND QUESTIONNAIRE THAT GENERATE RESPONSES

PICK THE RIGHT DATING SITE AND SEARCH FOR THE MEN WHO ARE PERFECT FOR YOU

THE OPENING PROFILE

HOW TO TURN A BROWSE INTO A CLICK

The opening profile is your first and perhaps most important dating tool. In this chapter, you'll learn how to avoid the mistakes made by 90 percent of searchers and create a profile that captures your strong points and stands out from the crowd.

ELEMENTS OF THE OPENER

As you'll see in chapter 6, there are many different sites to choose from, but almost all of them have a similar format. First, there's a browsing section (or opener) with lots of potential daters to scan. If an entry seems interesting, the browser can click it to reach the second section, a fleshed-out questionnaire that reveals more about that person.

Online browsers are busy and finicky. You have to grab their interest quickly so that they'll take an extra moment to click to your questionnaire. Without a catchy opener, they'll just scroll past you to someone else.

There are five elements to the opener:

- ✦ User name
- ✦ Banner headline (or subject line)
- ✦ Short personal profile
- ✦ Photo
- ✦ Summary sell-line

Each of these is an essential tool to grab a browser's attention and sell yourself.

"Oh, no," I can hear you thinking right now. "I can't sell myself!"

You sound just like my friend Jean from chapter 3. But I bet you can sell yourself in a soft way. It's a skill you practice every single day when you, for example:

- ✦ Sweet-talk the receptionist into squeezing you in for an appointment
- ✦ Show the boss that you're hardworking and competent
- ✦ Smile at the clerk at the checkout counter
- ✦ Ask your child to do you a favor

In each of these instances, you're exercising your talent to communicate, persuade, and be likable. You do it without even thinking about it. You're a natural salesperson. Creating a winning opener is simply a matter of unleashing your innate salesmanship.

User Name

Every word counts in your opener, including your user name. Save Susan6134 for your office or home computer. Your dating "handle" should be anonymous yet descriptive. One study of perceptions in cyberspace demonstrated that selective nicknames or handles influence the impressions others develop of the person using them. These little words count!

What two or three words fit you to a tee?

You might want to zero in on an activity or interest, like I did with my online ID, GolfNut. Or consider HappyHiker, NauticalGal,

OutdoorLover, WalkingWoman, LineDancer, HistoryBuff, BirderChick, BridgeBelle, or HookedonBooks.

You may have a fascinating profession to brag about, as did PaleoGal, ArtLady, and Novelist53. Or you may possess intriguing physical attributes, like NordicBlondeBuddy, Blondie, Green eyedLady, OleBlueEyes, SunnySmiles, Dimpled&Adorable, PolishednPretty, CuteRedhead, and Brown-eyedGal.

Personality might be your strong suit: HeartofGold, Warm&Lively, ThoughtfulLady, Friendly&Affectionate, GreatListener, Spirited&Sensitive, CozyCharmer, FunFran, HappyGal, SueIsNice, SweetnShy. Good, honest humor also gets noticed. I chuckled when I read the refreshing MiddleageOverweightSchoolmarm.

Banner Headline (Subject Line)

Most sites have a banner headline with the profile—a six- to 12-word phrase that offers you a second chance to grab attention and sell *yourself*. Notice the emphasis on *yourself*. Don't use this important real estate to describe the person you're looking for. He will find you if you do your selling job.

Put modesty aside for 15 minutes and jot down your wonderful attributes. (For inspiration, use the words from your Love Stories in chapter 2, many of which are in the "Glossary of Great Words" on page 68.) If you find that difficult to do, think about how good friends would describe you. What's it like to be with you? Don't guess; ask them. Friends can offer a fresh perspective and may be much more objective about you than you are.

In your collection of compliments, be sure that there are adjectives emphasizing your joy and vitality—"love to laugh," "crazy about fishing." At this stage, what attracts is a happy, healthy person who's warm and open to men, and has enthusiasm about life. Here are some more examples:

PLAYFUL PETITE REDHEAD
LIVE WIRE SEEKS SPARKS

CUTE LADY WHO LOVES HOCKEY

GOOD COOK AND CUDDLER

HAVE YOU HAD YOUR GIGGLE TODAY?

LET'S HAVE FUN

ATTRACTIVE. ADVENTUROUS. ADORABLE.

TRAVEL GAL WANTS A PAL

You'll notice that good banner headlines are positive, interesting, and humorous. They keep things light. Donna Frank of Nashua, New

GLOSSARY OF GREAT WORDS

Active	Easygoing	Like to laugh	Sincere
Adorable	Emotionally intelligent	Lively	Slightly padded
Adventurous		Long legs	Slim
Affectionate	Enjoy each day	Love to pamper	Smart as a whip
Alluring	Exuberant	Loving	Spirited
Appreciative	Financially secure	Low maintenance	Sporty
Athletic	Fit	Loyal	Successful
Attentive	Friendly	Openhearted	Sweet
Attractive	Fun	Open-minded	Tender
Charming	Giving	Optimistic	Thoughtful
Cheerful	Good cook	Outgoing	Toned
Communicative	Grounded	Petite	Understanding
Complete package	Happy	Playful	Vibrant
Considerate	Healthy	Potentially wicked	Vivacious
Crazy about	Heart of gold	Practical	Voluptuous
Creative	Helluva cook	Pretty	Warm
Cuddly	High energy	Reliable	Witty
Curious	Honest	Responsive	Youthful
Delightful	Independent	Romantic	Zaftig
Dimpled	In shape	Sassy	
	Kind	Shapely	

Hampshire, attracted now-husband Eric's attention with her headline, "Modern-Day Elaine Seeking Her Seinfeld."

On the other hand, banner headlines that spook guys are heavy and hostile. Don't make these mistakes:

Asking too much too soon. Imagine writing a résumé in which you told your prospective employer that you were looking for lifetime employment with a guarantee of happiness. That would be an absurd request from someone you'd never met. Equally absurd are similar banner headlines, such as HUSBAND WANTED, SHARE MY SOUL, or SPEND THE NEXT 20 YEARS WITH ME. So are ones that ask a perfect stranger to be perpetually amusing: EXCITE ME or GIVE ME A LIFETIME OF LAUGHTER. These remind me of the *Seinfeld* episode in which New York Mets' first baseman Keith Hernandez asks Jerry to help him move. "I hardly know the guy," Jerry protests, and rightly so. Only someone you're very intimate with should be asked to do such heavy lifting.

Sounding too sexy. You don't want to come across as a cyber-tramp with headlines such as CHECK OUT ROOTY TOOTY BOOTY, LET'S MAKE MISCHIEF, PASSIONATE WOMAN, or 1 SEXY LADY NEEDS NAUGHTY GUY. You may be flooded with e-mail, but not the kind you want.

Sounding too romantic. You'll seem naive and vulnerable if you opt for headlines such as SEARCHING FOR MY KNIGHT IN SHINING ARMOR. Also trite and overused: MR. RIGHT, MR. WONDERFUL, THAT SPECIAL SOMEONE, ONE IN A MILLION, LOVE AT FIRST SIGHT, HEARTTHROB, PRINCE CHARMING.

Picking on men. Many women, perhaps inadvertently, allow male bashing to creep into their banner headlines. Okay, maybe in the past you were burned by men, but you need to decide now whether you want to date 'em or hate 'em. (Review the READY tips in chapter 1.) If you want a fresh start with an online romance, note that stereotyping men as dishonest and irresponsible is not an attraction magnet. The hostility repels the good guys as well as the bad. Men like women who like men. Check your banner headline for these kinds of subtle or outright hostile put-downs: ARE YOU ONE OF THE NICE GUYS?; BE HONEST; NO HEAD GAMES; NO JERKS ALLOWED; NO CRAZIES, PLEASE; R U NORMAL?; NO MORE B-S!

Short Personal Profile

It's less than 100 words—sometimes as few as 25—but this descriptive paragraph needs to convey the experience of you. A good way to accomplish that is to divide the profile between your physical description and personality, keeping in mind the two questions you need to answer in this short space: What am I like? What is it like to be with me? Here are a few tips to get you started.

Physical

Tell the truth. Some sites require you to disclose height, weight, and age right up front. If you've been fudging for a while and can get away with shaving a few pounds or years, you might be okay. But any experienced online dater will warn you that you're risking wrath when you lie. Clever explanations and apologies will *not* earn you forgiveness if

---

THE AGE ISSUE

Contrary to popular belief, most mature men don't want a younger woman. Statistically, they tend to marry women close to their own age. But women who age well or look young for their age seem to have the odds in their favor. In his study of marriage-minded men, author and image consultant John Molloy reports that a majority of men over 40 want a woman who is "going to stay in shape, keep her figure, and pay attention to her appearance." Molloy's survey, the subject of his book *Why Men Marry Some Women and Not Others*, also found that "half the men over 40 who have dated, lived with, or married much younger women would hesitate to do so again." ‣

you've wasted someone's time by misrepresenting yourself. When the 50-SOMETHING TENNIS CHAMP I agreed to meet turned out to be 72, the sweet bouquet he brought didn't keep me from leaving soon after our handshake. He'd insulted me by lying.

There's no reason to lie about your age. Why compromise your credibility when so many online searchers will treasure the years you're trying to hide? In chapter 6, you'll preview sites specifically for Boomers. The big sites, such as Match.com, Yahoo! Personals, or Matchmaker, also have millions of mature browsers and are experiencing double-digit growth in our demographic group.

Jim Fischer, who started his online search at 49, listed "someone my own age" as his number one criteria. "I was married for seven years to a Gen Xer who was 15 years younger than me," he says. "What a disaster! Her cultural references began with the movie *Sixteen Candles* and ended somewhere around *Buffy the Vampire Slayer*. I wanted someone on my level, someone without a tongue ring or tattoos and who could answer, 'Where were you when President Kennedy was assassinated?'"

There's also no reason to lie about your weight. Maybe you won't attract the guy who wants a perfect size six. Don't worry about him. You don't need to appeal to everyone. Set your sights on the person you really want to meet. Get his attention by describing yourself in flattering terms, such as BBW (big, beautiful woman), voluptuous, or sensuous size 16.

When Jim linked to Stephanie, now his wife, "we were both toting some extra pounds," he says. "That's called, 'you get older and you put on weight.' It's just life."

Use colorful language and humor. Instead of "tall," how about saying you're "long-legged"? The latter creates a more sensual mental picture, like Lauren Bacall showing off her great gams in *To Have and Have Not*. Instead of "brown hair with highlights," don't you think it would be more fun to meet a "nearly blonde dazzler"?

Personality

Share your interests. The way you spend your leisure time is one of the best indicators of your personality and values. (If you've been too busy for hobbies, you may want to consider rounding out your life; refer back to chapter 1 and see the appendix.) Write down the activities that show both your playful and serious sides.

Notice the balance in these short profiles:

"My smile is contagious and so is my energy. I'm a gym rat, chess player, and volunteer community gardener, and I read all the historical fiction I can get my hands on. Let's laugh together . . . "

"I've built the kind of life where I can travel and have a good time. I try to walk every morning, and love trips where I trek around the countryside. I think that's the best way to really see things up close, and I can take time to enjoy a magnificent view, whether I just stumble across it or admire it during lunch at a roadside café."

Notice the lack of balance in this one:

"Sometimes I spend too much time at work and leave out the relaxing pleasures of mowing the lawn and weeding the garden."

EDUCATION AND SUCCESS: THE HOT NEW TICKET

There's a shift in the marriage market, according to University of Texas professor Kelly Raley, Ph.D. In her study of marital preferences, based on data from the National Survey of Families and Households, Dr. Raley was surprised to find that men are *most* willing to marry women with more education and earning power than they have themselves. "Attractiveness may still be important," she says, "but it looks as if men want women with greater economic resources."

Another study, from the University of Utah, also confounded researchers. Contrary to predictions, the woman who described herself in an ad as "financially independent, successful (and) ambitious" generated twice as many responses as the description "lovely . . . very attractive and slim." ʞ

Appeal to your target audience. One of the fundamental rules in sales and marketing is to know to whom you're selling. In this instance, your goal is to appeal to a member of the opposite sex. The key word here is *opposite*. My gorgeous friend Marion wondered why she wasn't getting e-mail. Here's the line from her opening profile that killed her chances: "My favorite activity is shopping!!! I love clothes." This would be a great hook if she were hoping to land a woman friend. But in my experience, if you give a man a choice between shopping and having a root canal, the latter has a better chance of winning. (The exception, of course, would be helping a woman pick out a bathing suit—lots of male volunteers there.)

Too much domesticity can also turn off men. You're not applying for the job of cook, maid, or nanny. Clean out language that pigeonholes you as a housebound Heloise. Check, for example, that your list of activities includes more than cooking, gardening, needlepoint, crafts, and yard sales. You want to appear dynamic in a number of spheres.

This profile shows symmetry between domesticity and romance:

"I cook very well, especially if you'll share a good wine and talk with me while I'm marinating the steaks."

This one reaches domestic nirvana from a man's point of view:

"I am a very happy, low-maintenance person who enjoys simple pleasures like barbecuing on my deck as I watch the sun set over the golf course."

Offer specific, telling details. Most adults enjoy dinner, movies, music, and travel. It's the distinguishing detail that will catch the eye of your compatible partner. If nothing tastes better to you than a cold beer and a hot dog at the ballpark, say so. (Boy, will you get e-mail!) If you've seen every single Steven Spielberg movie, let the other Spielberg fans know. Tout your uniqueness and expertise with specifics:

"I was brought up on the Sound and know the waters south of Boston down to City Island pretty well."

Demonstrate what you're describing:

"Great sense of humor (think Robin Williams—only calmer)."

Or, as Eric Frank had Donna giggling:

"My friends think I'm funny (I love my friends)."

One detail you don't want to disclose in the opening profile is information on your family. Keep the first impression focused on you. No distractions—even lovable ones—just yet. Save the introduction to your family for the questionnaire or first date. Here's how bringing up the family too early can backfire:

If you write:	He'll think:
I have two daughters who are the love of my life.	I'll never come first.
Here's a photo of me with my sister in Paris. Every year we take a wonderful vacation together.	This sister is going to hate me stepping in. I see trouble.
My favorite place to relax is at my family's home in Connecticut.	Uh-oh. Wonder what they're like.

Avoid the negative. I believe honesty is the best policy—but not the despairing, soul-baring kind of honesty evident below. Would you respond to these women or flee?

"I'm tired of sitting at home waiting for Mr. Right to knock at my door, and I hate those singles bars. All my friends are married, and I feel like the third wheel. I need a life."

"I haven't worked in a while because I was badly injured when I fell down a flight of stairs. While I was recovering, I had to cope with a divorce. But now I'm ready for someone who can make me smile again."

No man in his right mind would want to shoulder that kind of burden. Guys are not online to do a rescue mission.

Demands can backfire, too. They turn off all men because they make you seem hard to please and testy. Don't say what you *don't* want.

"Don't answer this if you're not a gentleman."

"Game players need not apply!"

"I only want to hear from someone who wants to make a commitment."

A more positive approach would be:

"I would like to meet a friend who also likes to walk for exercise."

Defensiveness is another form of negativity. There's no need to feel bashful or ashamed about going online. Millions of smart, attractive people—including the men who'll be scanning your profile—have made cyber-dating a socially acceptable option. Congratulate yourself that you're healthy, confident, and savvy enough to take control of finding a loving relationship. Don't waste time and valuable words on apologies like these from . . .

The virgin searcher: "Well, I've never done this before and I'm not very good at it, but here goes. . . . "

The resigned searcher: "Nothing but sheer desperation has brought me here. I'm determined to meet that one guy in a million, the one who will fall in love with me at first sight."

The halfhearted searcher: "My sister talked me into this, and I have no idea what I'm doing."

Photo

Posting a photo on the opener is a must. Profiles with photos generate 80 percent more responses, according to site managers. Some women say they don't want to be judged by their photos. I would counter by saying that you won't be in the contest at all. "No pix, no picks" is how it's played. Not having a photo with your profile implies that you have something to hide. It's a caution flag. Think about it: Would *you* choose someone who didn't post a photo?

If the technical aspects bother you, note that sites now offer step-by-step instructions on how to get your picture online. If you have a digital camera, you're set. You can also get traditional photos inexpensively converted to digital at Wal-Mart, copy shops, or photo stores like Photomax. Some online sites, such as ThirdAgePersonals.com, will do all the work for you—you e-mail or mail them your photo, and they'll do the posting and/or digital conversion for you.

Which photo to choose?

Select a shot that offers the clearest, most flattering view of you. A professional head shot (if not too stiff—warmth is very important) works quite well. If you don't have one, consider having one made, and see if the photographer could recommend a hair-and-makeup person who can help you achieve a natural-but-gorgeous look. (This could be the best investment you ever make!)

A photo that shows a hint of location in the background also can be very engaging. But you—not the mountains, the seashore, or the Eiffel Tower—must be the star. In fact, your backyard on a sunny day may be all the location you need. Sit in a comfortable chair and ask the photographer to crop in on you from the waist up. Look relaxed and happy, and you've got the perfect pose.

You'll have a chance to include other pictures with your questionnaire. There you can show off how sexy you look in a ski outfit or what a knockout you are when dressed to the nines. But remember to keep the opening photo clear and simple. If a guy can't get a good look at you, he may skip to someone else. Other photo pointers:

↗ Avoid old photos. Never post anything more than two years old.

↗ Showing too much skin may send the wrong message about you. You don't want to attract a bad kind of guy.

↗ Try to project warmth, one of the characteristics mature men want most. A big smile and cozy sweater signal that you're kind-hearted; sunglasses say cool, not warm. My friend Hildy didn't want her doctorate degree to seem intimidating, so she included a shot showing her holding mother and baby sloths. Half her e-mailers skipped over the Ph.D. part. They wanted to know what the heck she had around her neck.

↗ Group photos are confusing. Maybe your hair did look fabulous on the night of your high school reunion, but the other folks in the photo are a distraction. Pick another good-hair moment.

✦ Don't crop your former husband or boyfriend out of a photo unless he won't be missed, because a strange arm around your shoulder that's not attached to a body looks very weird. The trace of an ex also suggests that you haven't moved on from that relationship. Haven't you had a good time since you two parted?

✦ Save photos of the kids for an in-person meeting.

Summary Sell-Line

After you've created a warm, interesting picture of yourself and posted an equally wonderful photo, it's time to clinch the click. The fifth step is a simple, very effective two-part sales strategy that will distinguish you from the crowd.

Offer what marketers call the value proposition. What's in it for the browser? What can you promise that will make him click on you and not the competition? Note how well this four-sentence summary sell-line states the value proposition and makes the case for a future relationship:

"I will be a good friend and ally. I will be tender, responsive, appreciative, agreeable. I will inspire you. I will listen to you."

WORK IN WORD

There are three good reasons to compose and save your profile in a word-processing program like Microsoft Word or Corel WordPerfect.

1. You can cut and paste the profile into applications on multiple sites—a shortcut you'll appreciate.

2. You'll have a chance to do a spelling-and-grammar check. Silly errors may raise questions about your intelligence.

3. Your profile can be updated with a few simple changes. Updating keeps your profile fresh, and with each update your ad gets reposted to the front of the queue of candidates, bettering your chances of getting noticed. If your ad has been up a month or more, an update is in order. ✦

Or this amusing proposition:

"I'm sweet, energetic and sexy, intelligent and ticklish. I love to learn and try new things, and I want the full experience. I will never call the psychic hotline. We could be crazy about each other."

Ask for the business. Invite the browser to discover more about you:

"My idea of a great companion is someone who has a strong identity, who's passionate about life and ready for a good thing. I can't wait to meet you."

"One warm heart deserves another. I want to know what stirs you; what brings you joy; what brings that smile to your face. Maybe we connect. Let's find out."

PUTTING IT ALL TOGETHER

Here are just a few profiles that combine all five elements in a short package. Examine them for a moment. Do you notice the descriptive detail, humor, warmth, sense of fun, and positive attitude? Do you think the user names and banner headlines will appeal to men? Can you find the value proposition in each? Underline the phrases that welcome more contact (that is, ask for the business).

5-MINUTE PROFILE MAKER

To get your creative juices flowing, visit www.AARPmagazine.org and click on "Lifestyle." The free, interactive Personal Ad Maker tool will ask you 15 questions and build an ad for you. The Personal Ad Maker, the Glossary of Great Words (page 68), and words from your Love Stories (chapter 2) are starting points, but your profile will be much more effective if it uniquely captures you in your own words.

Big sites, such as Match.com and PerfectMatch.com, help with the writing even as you compose. Plus, you can click to more tips on the site or even hire a profile-writing counselor for a fee. ProfileHelper.com also supplies profile makeovers for $29.95. eHow.com gives good free advice, but will not write or rewrite for you. ⬆

LuvsFootball

WANT TO CATCH A GAME WITH ME?

I'm a 1940s model equipped with many features: warmth, joy, adventurousness, interest in what you have to say, intelligence, humor, and a sensuous nature. I value great conversations, football tickets, and white pistachio nuts. I could be talked into giving up the nuts, but not the football! If you provide the tailgate for the game, I'll treat you to my spicy chicken wings.

DreamersGirl

KIND, SMART, SPIRITED, SOMETIMES SILLY.

There are many sides to me. I'm exciting, energetic, passionate, and also sensitive and sweet. I love dancing (you lead), fly fishing (I'm a beginner), and pampering people (I give great back rubs). My secret passion is watching classic movie comedies. I'm such a buff that I can recite whole skits, such as "Who's on First?" (But I won't until you ask me.) If you're a complex guy looking for an attractive, multifaceted woman, please e-mail me. I will not bore you.

Sunny&Cozy

WHY IS THIS WOMAN SMILING?

I am a slender, but not skinny, active woman who is a lotta fun to be with. I'm financially secure, wickedly witty, and have a creative career with lots of flexibility for travel. You can plunk me down in a bistro on the Left Bank or Porky's Barbecue on the Outer Banks, and I'll be happy. I'm hoping to hear from an agreeable companion with a nice face and optimistic outlook on life. I will never take my guy for granted.

⚜

See, this profile writing doesn't have to be so hard. I'll bet you can knock one out right now, maybe with a little help from the resources in this chapter. Enjoy thinking about yourself in a creative way, then move on to the questionnaire. You're almost finished with your dating tools!

5

THE ART OF ANSWERING THE QUESTIONNAIRE

The profile is the first way to grab a browser's attention. But if he likes your catchy headline, photo, and positive personality, he's going to want to know a lot more about you. That's where the second important dating tool comes into play. Your answers to the questionnaire continue to build your case, strengthening your appeal. The questionnaire helps him decide if you're interesting and compatible enough to risk contacting. It has another essential roles, as well. Many sites, as you'll learn in the next chapter, will offer to pair you up with candidates who seem right for you. To do that, they use information from your questionnaire, so don't take it lightly. Here are some questions you might encounter and a few ideas on answers.

BASIC STUFF

Almost every site will ask about your age, children, education, occupation, religion, ethnicity, height, and weight. Be absolutely honest. You can't recover from misrepresenting yourself.

Other boilerplate questions are not as simple to answer. You may not want to disclose your income, for example. You may not know how to describe your body type. A question about marital status can also be tricky if you're in a transitional state. Some ways to handle these:

The income dodge. Most sites let you off the hook on this sensitive question. They offer answers for you, such as "only my accountant knows," "I'll tell you when we meet," or "no answer." These are sensible and safe replies.

Money does have its charm, however, and studies show that men these days find wealth and success very charming qualities indeed (see

STIR UP TV MEMORIES

Almost every Q&A has a section where you tell how you entertain yourself. I'm not good at this. I forget movies, shows, even books I've read, unless I'm reminded. So I've included some helpful hints throughout this chapter for Boomers who have memories like mine. Why not include a mix of oldies along with new shows?

Baby Boomers' Headquarters—BBHQ.com—polls members on favorite TV shows, songs, and movies, and is a storehouse of Boomer trivia. Do any of these shows ring a bell?

Ben Casey	My Favorite Martian
Branded	The Pinky Lee Show
Car 54, Where Are You?	The Real McCoys
The Cisco Kid	The Rifleman
Davy Crockett	Sea Hunt
Fury	77 Sunset Strip
Have Gun—Will Travel	Sky King
The Life and Legend of Wyatt Earp	Topper
The Life of Riley	The Untouchables
The Many Loves of Dobie Gillis	Zorro
Mister Ed	

Do you want to know the cast list for *Yancy Derringer*? Remember who played Congressman Glen Morley in *The Farmer's Daughter*? Check out www.MemorableTV.com.

"Education and Success: The Hot New Ticket" on page 72). It's your call what to disclose, but don't be so boastful as to discourage suitors or encourage predators.

Is any body perfect? I hate the question on body type. The kindest words for this Q may be descriptors such as "average," "ample," "large." Don't fall for the characterization "thick."

Marital status. Many dating sites offer options for players and marital cheats. They can select the "hot" or "intimate" buttons and get directed to like-minded partners. It's also easy for someone contemplating a breakup to browse and see what's out there. Most online daters would agree that players and browsers should not post and pretend to be single or ready for commitment. That's deceptive.

Then there's the gray area of people who are separated. Many sites will not let you search with the singles if you're in this ambiguous position. You can look for a "friend," "pen pal," or "activity partner," but not someone to date or marry. Some sites, in fact, are beginning to verify members' matrimonial status (see chapter 6). Here's the rub: divorce takes time—years, even—and you may not want to hobble your social life while you wait for an official decree. My suggestion: Read the site's FAQs about marital status to get a sense of how strict they are. Will you be allowed to search the better database of singles if you indicate you're separated? Can you take a chance on checking "divorced" if that's closer to the real status (you're not living together, and papers have been filed)?

QUESTIONS THAT REVEAL MORE ABOUT YOU

"Some people play hard to get. I play hard to want."
—Andrew Dice Clay, *The Adventures of Ford Fairlane*

Some sites set you up on the dating express with very little information. Simply supply the Basic Stuff, a zip code—maybe your astrological sign—and you're good to go. They'll send you a pick of all the Libras your age in the neighborhood. A really good match, however, requires more information from you, along with thought and time.

(continued on page 86)

TOP TUNES FOR BOOMERS

Visitors to BBHQ.com voted for these favorite songs, Also check out iTunes.com for the latest music.

Song	Artist
"American Pie"	Don McLean
"Born to Be Wild"	Steppenwolf
"Bridge Over Troubled Water"	Simon & Garfunkel
"California Dreamin'"	The Mamas and the Papas
"Chances Are"	Johnny Mathis
"Cherish"	The Association
"Good Vibrations"	The Beach Boys
"Hey Jude"	The Beatles
"The House of the Rising Sun"	The Animals
"Layla"	Eric Clapton
"Leaving on a Jet Plane"	Peter, Paul & Mary
"Light My Fire"	The Doors
"Mack the Knife"	Bobby Darin
"Maggie May"	Rod Stewart
"Me and Bobby McGee"	Janis Joplin
"Only the Lonely"	Roy Orbison
"(I Can't Get No) Satisfaction"	The Rolling Stones
"Sounds of Silence"	Simon & Garfunkel
"Stairway to Heaven"	Led Zeppelin
"Summer in the City"	Lovin' Spoonful
"This Girl is a Woman Now"	Gary Puckett & the Union Gap
"Unchained Melody"	The Righteous Brothers
"White Rabbit"	Jefferson Airplane
"Yesterday"	The Beatles

MOVIE TIME

Your favorite flicks tend to be weepies like *Steel Magnolias* or *Beaches*. He's more of a *Bourne Supremacy*, *Gladiator*, and *Saving Private Ryan* kind of guy. Critically acclaimed movies can balance things out. Here's a list of 100 Most Acclaimed Movies from CinePad.com. It's compiled from a number of critics' choices, such as the American Film Institute, National Film Registry, and National Society of Film Critics. I've listed them alphabetically.

The African Queen	*Dr. Strangelove*
All About Eve	*Duck Soup*
All Quiet on the Western Front	*E.T.—The Extra-Terrestrial*
Amadeus	*Fantasia*
American Graffiti	*Fargo*
An American in Paris	*Forrest Gump*
Annie Hall	*Frankenstein*
The Apartment	*The French Connection*
Around the World in 80 Days	*From Here to Eternity*
Atlantic City	*The General*
Ben-Hur	*Gigi*
The Best Years of Our Lives	*The Godfather*
Bonnie and Clyde	*The Godfather, Part II*
Bringing Up Baby	*The Gold Rush*
Casablanca	*Gone with the Wind*
Chinatown	*GoodFellas*
Citizen Kane	*The Graduate*
City Lights	*Greed*
A Clockwork Orange	*High Noon*
Dances with Wolves	*How Green Was My Valley*
The Deer Hunter	*In the Heat of the Night*
Double Indemnity	*Intolerance*

It Happened One Night	Platoon
It's a Wonderful Life	Psycho
The Jazz Singer	Pulp Fiction
King Kong	Raging Bull
Kramer vs. Kramer	Rear Window
L.A. Confidential	Rebel Without a Cause
Leaving Las Vegas	Rocky
The Life of Emile Zola	The Rules of the Game
The Lost Weekend	Schindler's List
Louisiana Story	The Searchers
The Magnificent Ambersons	Shane
The Maltese Falcon	The Silence of the Lambs
The Manchurian Candidate	Singin' in the Rain
Marty	Snow White and the Seven Dwarfs
M*A*S*H	Some Like It Hot
Midnight Cowboy	The Sound of Music
Modern Times	Star Wars
Mr. Smith Goes to Washington	A Streetcar Named Desire
Mutiny on the Bounty	Taxi Driver
My Fair Lady	Terms of Endearment
Nashville	Tootsie
Network	The Treasure of the Sierra Madre
North by Northwest	Unforgiven
One Flew Over the Cuckoo's Nest	Vertigo
On the Waterfront	West Side Story
Ordinary People	The Wizard of Oz
Patton	Wuthering Heights
A Place in the Sun	Yankee Doodle Dandy

I'm biased, of course, in favor of the more detailed approach. I think it saves effort in the long run to go for quality candidates on quality sites. But let's make the whole business easier on you. Here's a crib sheet to help you score better with your responses to more comprehensive questions. And remember, whether you're checking a multiple-choice answer or writing about yourself or interests, you're creating an impression. Resist sarcasm and the temptation to be coy with a lot of "tell ya later's"—there may not be a later if you come across as tough or withholding.

Health habits. If you indicate that you smoke, your number of replies will be lower. Forget about fudging this answer, however. You can't hide a smoking habit from a nonsmoker after you meet. It's better to be honest and hope you find a Marlboro man to light up your life. As for the other common vice, alcohol, "moderate drinking" is probably the answer most people pick, except on religious sites. Fitness (not fanaticism) and healthy eating (mostly) show that you take care of yourself but are not uptight about it. As one profiler put it, "I prefer to be healthy, but I'm not afraid of a little debauchery."

Pets. Millions of singles have pets; and millions of singles are allergic or have an aversion to pets. Sometimes you can work it out. (I knew Walter was seriously committed, for example, when he gave his cat to his daughter, Renie, because I was so allergic.) But sometimes pets are a deal breaker for a potential match. If you have a whole bunch of critters—say, three or more cats and dogs, or a herd of pot-bellied pigs—you may want to try one of the sites especially for pet lovers (see page 100).

Politics. Life could be easier, choices more plentiful, if you consider yourself a political moderate. If you're a Democrat, for example, does that mean you'll rule out all Republicans? Be sure your answers don't hamstring you. On the other hand, you need to be yourself, and if you have strong opinions, left or right, you could get the vote of someone who shares your very same views.

Clocks and body clocks. If you're punctual, try not to appear as if you're rigid about it. "Usually on time" is a very human answer. Night owls may as well fess up. You won't be able to fool someone who turns in at 10 every night.

Where you live, have lived, or want to live. Descriptions of your home create a feeling about you. Feed the imagination with your prose. Do you live in a large, roomy place with a yard big enough to house your prize roses or tomatoes? Maybe your space is small and cozy, packed with books, art, and a piano that barely squeezes into the living room. It could be modern and tidy —lots of sunshine, high ceilings, minimal clutter. Describe your favorite room: What's on the wall in your bedroom? What's your kitchen like (and what's in the fridge)? Use adjectives that evoke the five senses.

Also use rich detail if asked to describe your kind of town or city. What's charming about your neighborhood? Where are the best places to have fun? Don't miss a chance to talk about your old stomping grounds. Charlene Black in Greenwood, South Carolina, replied to a message from her now husband, Steve, because she noticed in his questionnaire that he was originally from her hometown. And where would you like to be down the road: in a golf villa at Hilton Head, a cabin in the Smokies, or a loft in the city? Boomers like to fantasize about relocating.

Interests and Activities

> "All a man wants is a little fun."
> —Brian Ahern, *The Best of Everything*

Some sites will ask you to check off your favorite recreational and leisure activities. I've discovered that it's better to limit the choices to three or four, definitely no more than six. My reason is simple: I think some search engines weigh this section too heavily. One site I researched, for example, e-mailed me a prospect that was supposed to be a 100 percent match. I couldn't figure out how this smoker who never exercised and lived at the outer border of my geographic range would get such a high score. I realized I had overemphasized activities on my form. Like the alleged 100 percent match, I had checked bingo, which I play about once every 10 years if I happen to be on a cruise ship. Yes, I like bingo, but it's not a higher priority than nonsmoking.

In addition to checking off activities, you may be asked brief essay-type questions such as "What do you do for fun?" and "Why you should get to know me." Again, remember that your audience is male. If you go on and on about shopping, manicures, and crafts, you may not find as many takers. Also, be sure to add the telling details that make you interesting, good company, and unique.

FAMOUS MOVIE LINES

"What do you want me to do, draw you a picture, spell it out?"
—John Wayne, *The Searchers* (1956)

Okay, I will spell it out. You can find a fabulous database of great movie lines at ReelComments.com. (I couldn't resist using a few in this chapter.) Quotes really perk up questionnaires and e-mails. The site also lists best comedies, horror movies, disaster flicks, and the kind of war stories and cop films men tend to enjoy. It wouldn't hurt to sprinkle a "guy flick" or two into your questionnaire.

Top 10 War Movies	Top 10 Cop Movies
Saving Private Ryan	*Die Hard with a Vengeance*
Platoon	*The Fugitive*
Good Morning, Vietnam	*Basic Instinct*
Apocalypse Now	*Se7en*
*M*A*S*H*	*Lethal Weapon 3*
Patton	*Beverly Hills Cop*
The Deer Hunter	*Beverly Hills Cop II*
Full Metal Jacket	*Lethal Weapon 4*
Midway	*Speed*
The Dirty Dozen	*Lethal Weapon 2*

- "I can recite Chaucer in Middle English for that hot English major foreplay."
- "I like to have adventures, big or small."
- "I walk six miles per day and would like a companion to share stories with as well as the miles."
- "You should get to know me because I'm fun and funny and have the whitest hair you've ever seen, and because travel is my passion (I'm a duffel-bag lady)."
- "I am independent and have an active civic and social life, but am hoping to find someone who will give me a reason to stay home from time to time."

Whom Am I Looking For?

"I made a resolution never again to take up
with any hell-bent types."
—Sissy Spacek, *Badlands*

Don't use romantic shorthand and answer this essay-type question by saying "Prince Charming" or "My Knight in Shining Armor." Use the words you discovered in the worksheets in chapter 2. What are the five (or so) bottom-line qualities in a man that make you happy to be with him? Here's how some online daters answered.

I want someone who is . . .

- . . . smart, funny, kind, notices the little things about me, and likes to talk or not talk for hours.
- . . . open-minded, adventurous, loves the outdoors, and is engaged in the world. Someone nice who has a sense of humor.
- . . . strongly masculine (not brutish) and wants to do things, see things, and experience as much as possible. Someone offbeat, communicative, and emotionally intelligent.

Personality profiles on Match.com and PerfectMatch.com can also help define the person you want (see chapters 4 and 6). Here's an edited version of my personality results from PerfectMatch.com: "I'm a cautious optimist who takes time for love, and I need someone with the same priority. I also need growth, change, and, perhaps, adventure, and want to be with someone who desires, like me, to keep life and relationships stimulating and new."

The Food Connection

Dining out is one of the most popular dates, and writing about the foods you love reveals a lot about your background, passions, and personality. I like the way the Match.com questionnaire prompts members to discuss favorite local hot spots. It's a super icebreaker that builds points of connection. Collect a list of the best:

- Gourmet spot with harbor view
- Cozy country inn
- Hamburger dive with amazing jukebox
- Brick-oven pizzeria

BOOK NOTES

List all-time favorites, as well as something new. Include fiction and non-fiction. I'd save Jane Austen or romance novels until after the marriage. Also steer clear of political titles, unless you're proclaiming a left-wing or right-wing leaning. The number one best seller is inevitably overused, but I found this profile's recommendation somewhat intriguing: "If you liked *The Da Vinci Code*, read the more interesting *Holy Blood, Holy Grail* by Michael Baigent." And don't forget the books that make you laugh out loud—you may want to share a line or two to illustrate what amuses you. An online book club at SeniorNet.com discusses favorite choices of members.

- Deli for Philly cheesesteaks, falafel, hoagies, or Cuban sandwiches
- Hangout for lobster rolls, shrimp po'boys, conch fritters

Food is fun to write about and discuss. My husband and I can while away the hours of a car trip deconstructing the chopped barbecue sandwiches we once ate in Wilkesboro, North Carolina. We spent two years discussing Varsity hot dogs in Atlanta versus Dew Drop Inn hot dogs in Mobile. He finally moved to the Dew Drop side, so now we simply reminisce obsessively over the top dog. (No letters, please. Atlanta's Colonnade still wins hands down in the coconut-cream pie division of our food fantasies.) Even if you're strictly a meat-and-potatoes sort, where do you get those marbled strip steaks, cooked just right, and those fresh, crisp, salty fries?

Questionnaires differ from site to site, but reviewing this chapter will give you a heads-up on most of the questions you'll encounter. It's almost like prepping for a job interview—you want good answers ready. With your two dating tools—the profile and questionnaire—prepared in advance, you'll have an easy time searching and posting on a number of fabulous sites, coming up next!

6

THE RIGHT SITE

"Much as the automobile revolutionized dating in the 1920s and the birth control pill transformed mating in the 1960s, the Internet has reshaped the relationships of today. It's a watershed moment in the history of courtship," according to social historian Barbara Defoe Whitehead.

Internet dating sites are booming. There are tens of thousands to choose from, and new ones start up every day. Not to worry, though. It's easy to whittle down the choices. Eliminate all the sites for Russian and Asian brides, swingers, kooks, and people under 30, and there's a reasonable number to work with.

The two lists in this chapter will save you time. The first comprises Big Favorites—the best known, most reputable sites with over one million members. The second list describes Special Appeal sites—those with a smaller but distinctive membership base. Let's start with the Big Favorites. Here are the criteria I used to select these sites:

Viability. Online dating is big business, a $450 million category in 2003. Small services are being gobbled up by big ones or closing up shop literally overnight. The Big Favorite picks have the best chance of staying live.

Techno appeal. The Big Favorites have incredible technology, graphics, and customer service. In this highly competitive market, top sites constantly add value in an attempt to gain you as a customer. The

Special Appeal list focuses on smaller, specialized services that vary greatly in their technical capabilities.

Quantity and quality. Big Favorites have a large number of candidates in the 35-to-64 age range. Their numbers are so big, in fact, that you often can be selective on a number of important criteria—not only age and location but also personality, activities, and religious preference, for example. Special Appeal sites will yield fewer choices, but each one may be closer to what you want.

Reputation. To get the lowdown on Big Favorites, I read hundreds of Web logs, or "blogs," about online dating sites and reviews posted on eDateReview.com. One expensive, well-known site—with a $10 million ad campaign—had such poor word of mouth that I dropped it from the original list. You can do a fresh investigation on your own by typing in "complaints about [the name of your site]" in the bar of your search engine. Because of their size, Special Appeal sites don't generate as much attention, positive or negative, so be sure to study their statements about customer service, safety, and privacy.

WHERE TO BEGIN

Most sites permit browsing to whet your appetite for a full-fledged search. Take advantage of this free offer, as it's a good way to get a sense of the men you'll meet on that site. Remember, however, that a browse is not a search. It's more like coming attractions at the movies—just a hint of what you'll find.

Even if you're doing a little site seeing, with no plans to enroll, be prepared with your profile, photo, and sample answers for a questionnaire. You never know when you're going to be impressed, and you may want to sign up on the spot. Why miss out on a great opportunity? Have your dating tools ready.

Most online daters are faithful to a particular site. At first you, too, may want to rely on just one, until you're comfortable with the process.

Then you should improve your chances by eventually adding one or two others—a second Big Favorite and perhaps a Special Appeal site.

Big Favorites (One Million-Plus Members)

Match.com. One of the largest and best, Match.com updates and upgrades constantly, raising the bar for other dating services. It claims that more than 200,000 members have found the person they're looking for.

With millions of members and enrollment fees starting at $30 per month, Match.com is a popular, long-term player. Over the last decade it has added to the family with kiss.com and udate.com (a sister site), and it's the premier provider of personals for Love@AOL, CompuServe, and Netscape.com.

Wow! This graphically attractive site offers every bell and whistle yet invented, and the customer-support services will walk you through how to set up and use it all. If you're interested in video capabilities, for example, you get step-by-step instructions and a member's discount on three types of desktop Webcams. Other tech options available:

- Voice greetings set up from your home phone. It's as easy as leaving a message on your answering machine.
- Match Mobile. Your profile can be transferred to your cell phone, and you can connect anonymously with singles near you. (Frankly, I think this is a feature for the young and restless.)
- Video greetings and live video. This removes some of the mystery and magic of e-mail correspondence (see chapter 8). To appear at your best, you need to be creative and at ease in front of the camera. On the other hand, if you hate surprises, this could be perfect for you.
- Online speed matching. This is a more convenient, more private form of speed dating. In speed dating, you might go to a prearranged restaurant and move from table to table every few min-

utes to meet different men. Online speed matching is over the phone in your own home. You register online for a local (one of 50 cities) or national session. You can also be broken down further into subgroups. New York–area singles, for example, could attend phone events sorted by age group, religion, or ethnicity. It's also possible to connect with outdoor lovers, animal lovers, or travel lovers, the marriage-minded, the recently divorced, or single parents. During a session you talk by phone to a date for four minutes while each of your photos is visible on the computer screen. You then see a scorecard to rate each other yes or no for follow-up contact. The next date, with someone else, begins a minute later. You may have from four to eight speed dates a session.

If you're not keen on dealing with high tech yourself, you may enjoy Match.com's innovations that require little from you. Their personality test is free for members and, mercifully, takes just a few minutes. The unique, free physical-attraction test is incredible. You're shown a series of photos of realistic-looking models' faces and physiques, and gradually narrow down the selections to your type. Some kind of face- and body-recognition wizardry then finds your type from the database of real people. Match.com also offers key words to help you refine a quick search, a flirting feature (winks), and organization strategies.

Match.com, which has as many as 29.6 million unique visitors each month, is welcoming to mature daters. You'll see photos and lots of testimonials from silver-haired singles. Match Live—the events arm of the company—sponsors get-togethers in urban areas such as New York City, Boston, Los Angeles, Chicago, and San Francisco. Recent samplings included mature-oriented workshops on swing dancing, shag dancing, wine tasting, and martini making. Match Travel offers 60 vacation offerings, many targeted to Boomers and single parents.

Match.com's innovations and customer service make it a leader. The site also has integrity. When I tested their searching and defined myself as being in a relationship, I was blocked from the actively dating singles sections. I liked that, even though it may cost the site some customers with cheating hearts. In fact, Match.com refuses to post an average of 3,000 profiles a month for those who do not meet their standards, such as people trying to post sexually explicit photos.

Yahoo! Personals and ThirdAge Personals. Huge, inexpensive ($20 a month), and easy to maneuver, Yahoo! Personals is a great site to begin with: they're extremely generous about free browsing and searching, and will even search for you at no cost. ThirdAge Personals, the site's co-branded partner, is customized specifically for people in midlife.

At just over 18 percent, Yahoo! Personals is the leader in market share for online dating services, according to Hitwise Competitive Intelligence (January 2004). ThirdAge Personals, formerly ThirdAge Connections, is a premier dating site for the mature market. Not as urban-oriented or slick as Match.com, Yahoo! Personals will fulfill your geographic desires, with abundant choices all over the country. Yahoo! Personals has about 6.2 million visitors each month, and ThirdAge Personals has over 20 million page views each month—that's *millions* of potential matches between these two services.

The Yahoo! and ThirdAge partnership is a win/win for Boomers. ThirdAge benefits from a redesign and techno improvements. Both services now have a large consolidated database of mature singles. If you begin your search on ThirdAge Personals, however, you'll also have the added benefit of articles and advice geared to Boomers. The ThirdAge newsletter, for example, carries up-to-the-minute features such as lowering cholesterol with cinnamon, teaching kids fiscal responsibility, and feeling fit after 40; plus, it offers specialized dating advice, such as "Relationships: Then vs. Now," "Confidence Corner," and "How You Can Trust Again."

Both Yahoo! Personals and ThirdAge Personals have the techno features you'll find on most good sites, such as voice and video greetings, a keyword search, and electronic flirting that sends an icebreaker message to a potential love interest. An organizing bar helps save searches and keep your love life straight.

The slide-show and photo-gallery views show multiple photos of a contact. Two interesting, convenient innovations are "attach a snapshot" and "affinity matching." The first lets you include a mini version of your ad when you respond, saving a lot of back-and-forth effort. Great advantage! Affinity matching is a super search feature. If you liked one profile, it will show you similar prospects, or "likely likeables," as they call it.

Yahoo! Personals and ThirdAge Personals have exceptional customer service. They seem to understand that mid-agers may not be as adept at technology as Gen Ys, and they go out of their way to make everything easy. Yahoo!

Matchmaker.com. At 18-plus years, Matchmaker is one of the oldest leading online dating services, with an estimated eight million active users. Although not as technologically or graphically up-to-date as Match.com and Yahoo! Personals, Matchmaker does offer standard features such as voice greetings, instant messaging, and an electronic flirting feature called a "wink" to alert prospects of your interest. Organizing tools include Hot List and a Matchmaker Diary to store your personal notes about contacts.

The best thing about Matchmaker is that it lives up to its name, as I can personally attest. Their MatchMeter system tells how good a match someone is for you. It worked incredibly well for me six years ago, when it rated my husband as highest in compatibility, and when I tested their approach recently, I found that it still knows how to pick potential

OTHER BIG FAVORITES

AmericanSingles.com. Certainly a popular site, with an estimated eight million members and features such as instant messaging and real-time chat. The site, however, doesn't seem as innovative or thoughtful as my favorites.

DreamMates.com. My in-box filled up every day with selections sent by DreamMates during a free trial. Volume was high, but not always on target. DreamMates has about 2.5 million members.

partners. Although my free trial didn't generate a mass of matches, each possibility seemed right on the mark.

Like the other Big Favorites, Matchmaker offers security for credit-card purchases, good customer service, and a blocking feature if you want to decline contact with an e-mailer.

PerfectMatch.com. Launched in August 2003, PerfectMatch is a newcomer that has already proven its popularity. It's beautifully designed and easy to maneuver. The focus is not on casual dating, as they state: "PerfectMatch.com is a community of serious committed adults looking for a long-term relationship."

Although young, PerfectMatch has experienced hands at the wheel. The CEO, Duane Dahl, was former CEO of kiss.com and udate.com (both now part of Match.com). The sociologist in residence, Pepper Schwartz, Ph.D., is a well-known relationship expert with real academic credentials (from Yale), research, and popular books to her credit. Last but not least, PerfectMatch has a long-term partnership with Lifetime Television to build and promote both brands.

Already at one million members, PerfectMatch is one of the fastest-growing sites, and Lifetime Television sends in a steady stream of new members. A downside of the Lifetime pool is that, unlike most sites, the skew is toward more women than men (65 percent to 35 percent). I suspect this will correct as more men discover the demographics. When you read online dating blogs, one of the chief beefs among guys is that there aren't enough women on some sites. PerfectMatch overcompensates for the inequity.

PerfectMatch has focused its technology on the personality assessment, profile, an ice-breaker option, and search.

↗ Personality assessment. This test, called Duet, was adapted by Dr. Schwartz (known on-site as Dr. Pepper) from a Myers-Briggs Type Indicator. The assessment explains personality types, an important part of matching, and instantly summarizes your personal results. My free test gauged me an XBOV—risk averse, relaxed, optimistic, seeks variety—which is true, and determined that only a third of members would be attracted to the likes of me. The test goes on to tell which traits your partner should share and which should be different.

↗ The well-organized profile. PerfectMatch's includes information on appearance, lifestyle, values, likes and dislikes, answers to insightful questions, and photos. The best features in this section are profile-improvement tips that coach you as you write and automatic spell-check—these would be welcome features on all sites. Premium members can also opt for more hands-on coaching from counselors with a 10 point profile review and tune-up.

↗ Icebreakers If you're shy about asking questions or not sure of what to ask, two levels of Ice Breakers can help you out. In an early stage of e-mail, for example, you can click and pose questions, such as "How would you describe your best (best) friend?" or "How often do you find yourself laughing?" Deal Breakers, another automatic option, make your minimum standards clear. These features save you from looking as if you're aggressive or overly picky. It's not you—it's the system.

↗ In-depth search. PerfectMatch does not promise a fast match or vast numbers because the criteria analyze more than zip codes. If you get antsy while awaiting their perfect matches, however, they will let you search on your own in several ways. You can try your own search based on personality or similarity and complementary factors, a keyword search, or an advanced-customized search. This freedom is a key benefit.

The founders of PerfectMatch started out doing things right, and the site is very woman-friendly, a lot like Lifetime Television. Dr. Schwartz's influence makes a big difference. She's a true expert, and a user gets a sense of her insight and reassuring support throughout. PerfectMatch employs the latest security and privacy technology. The SmutBot screens out inappropriate adult content.

Special Appeal Sites

Searching a big site is like shopping in a department store—lots of choices and something for almost everyone. The better big sites, such as Match.com and Yahoo! Personals, make a special effort to cater to different needs, such as mature singles or single parents. Sometimes, though, you want the boutique experience. A common factor—whether it's religion, age, ethnic background, or a love of pets—is essential to your happiness, and you're sure of what you want. These sites may help you find your reference group.

Age-Specific Sites

SeniorFriendFinder.com. From the same company that launched the popular FriendFinder.com, this sibling site draws about 300,000 members ages 30 to 90; the heart of the market, however, is the 45-to-55 group. The site's handle is "Dating for people with experience." The founder and CEO, Andrew Conru, Ph.D., characterizes the members as "more frank and honest and direct" than ones on other dating services. "They sure don't beat around the bush," he says.

SeniorFriendFinder offers full safety features, including the ability to block or report abusers and control access to personal information, as well as a system to confirm someone's identity. Tech features such as video greetings are available, although most members stick to digital photos. The 100-person customer-service center is available to assist with posting photos or profile writing for a $40 to $50 fee.

Also take a look at some of the smaller sites that specialize in mature romance, including SeniorDatefinder.com, primesingles.com, and Overfifties.com (more chat than dating service). And don't forget ThirdAge Personals (page 96).

Animal- and Pet-Related Sites

AnimalAttraction.com. The scuttlebutt is that places for pet lovers make good matches. Thus, there are a number of similar-minded sites.

Animal Attraction distinguishes itself by providing pet-care tips from the Humane Society of the United States. Otherwise the services seem remarkably alike, and pets are not restricted to dogs and cats. Even KissyKat.com is open to birds, fish, hamsters, ferrets, iguanas, and pot-bellied pigs.

Other contenders in this category include LoveMeLoveMyPets.com (one of the leading sites), DateMyPet.com (set up dates for you or your pets), and AnimalPeople.com (you don't have to have a pet, just a desire to connect with other animal lovers).

For horse enthusiasts, EquestrianSingles.com claims to be "the classiest online equestrian community," uniting riders around the world. There's also HorseLoversConnection.com, a site that lets you search for a partner with a similar style of riding (Western or English) and type of riding (pleasure/trail or competitive).

Country-Type Sites

CountrySingles.com. Originating as newspaper personals 17 years ago, CountrySingles still has a newspaper feel to it. The men, mostly from the Midwest, are refreshing in their honesty and open to all ages and types of women. One "self-reliant, hard-working" Minnesotan asked for a good-natured, healthy woman in the 30- to 60-year range. A 45-year-old in Wisconsin wrote, "Appearance isn't important. Race is open. Must be willing to relocate, however." Country Singles also links to 18WheelSingles.com.

CountryWesternSingles.com. I love this site! These straightforward cowboys love to cook and dance, and have real romance and poetry in their souls. They're plenty fit and good-looking, too. Just check out some sample profiles (as written) from men ages 45 to 64, and see what this site has to offer:

> ♦ "I am easy to get along with, passive, don't like to argue, like to enjoy life and have fun. Love to fish, rodeos, horses, picnic, moonlight rides, laying next to a fire with someone special."

- ✦ "I've been a cowboy all my life. A good one the last 40 years. I live on a ranch that has been in my family over 100 years. As far as looks go, I'm not too bad looking, but I am not Brad Pitt either."
- ✦ "I am easy going and a lot of fun to be with, I have a great sense of humor. I am a part time team roper and I love to dance. I love to travel and I try to treat a lady like a queen."
- ✦ "I am 62, in good health. I enjoy trail riding, hunting, fishing, target shooting, horse camping, the outdoors, country living, small town living. I retire in a couple of years and want to enjoy my life with a country type lady."
- ✦ "I love the cowboy/outdoors way of life and love to ride and pack. I am a good all around/handyman type of guy. Am a little shy but real easy to get along with. I love what I do and I love my mules too!!"
- ✦ "I enjoy taking care of animals and some people."
- ✦ "I love romance, snuggling, smooching and spooning."
- ✦ "I write poetry, play the guitar and sing."
- ✦ "Rancher ready to tie the knot."

Ivy League–Style

GoodGenes.com. No, you don't have to furnish a DNA sample or genealogy chart, but Good Genes is picky about the schools you attended. My alma mater didn't make the cut, but if you were an Ivy Leaguer or went to a good private college, they'll probably let you in the portal. In any case, it's fun to see what the guys from Harvard and other Ivies have been up to all these decades. Excerpts from profiles:

- ✦ "Humorous, socially conscious, altruistic, metaphysical, adventurous, good sense of the absurd, wry, cuddly, easily bored with trivia. Do not ski, play tennis or play golf or want to hear about it. Was once however a good ping pong player in college."

- "First from line of Irish brawlers to graduate from college. Bent my young passion to football, now politics and law. Even temperament; quick to smile."
- "Daughters tell me I'm not bad looking for an elderly man. Former altar boy, now lapsed Catholic. Retired Bonnie Raitt Groupie. Left-wing curmudgeon."
- "Interested in literature, philosophy, economics, music, theatre and the outdoors. Dante freak."
- "Professor seeks mature, reflective woman, liberal (may be feminist), sociable (not butterfly), fit, normal ht/wt, not fixed on dogma or ritual, dependents (if any) flown the coop."

Arty/Urban Sites

Nerve.com. A "smart, honest magazine on sex," according to their self-description, Nerve also has an active personals section which, when I checked it out, has cute guys our age. The writing tends to be cool and amusing, and may offer some inspiration to zip up your own. One guy, for example, answered the question "Celebrity I most resemble" with "Woody Woodpecker." Another did this riff on the question:

"Paul McCartney meets John Steed meets Bruce Lee meets Morey Amsterdam meets Chevy Chase meets Jackson Browne meets Hunter Thompson meets Bob Weir meets George Clooney meets Inspector Clouseau."

The most amusing part is that the answers of both men were remarkably accurate descriptions.

Also in this arty, irreverent category: Bust.com.

Race- or Ethnic-Specific Sites

BlackSingles.com. Billing itself as "the world's largest singles network for people of color," BlackSingles.com has more than 300,000 registered members. The online social community also hosts events, including an annual singles cruise. Its competitors include BlackPlanetLove.com and BlackSinglesConnection.com.

LatinoPeopleMeet.com caters to 10 different ethnicities and offers video and voice greetings. MiGente.com has broader appeal—24 Hispanic ethnic origins, six sections for race, and 18 religious choices. The wonderful diversity of MiGente.com, however, is marred by pop-up ads and advertisements.

Click2Asia.com. A socially active site, Click2Asia promotes lots of live events, like comedy-club outings and speed dating in Los Angeles, New York City, and San Jose. Its competitors include AsiaFriendFinder.com, AsianSinglesConnection.com, and, for those of Muslim, Hindu, or Sikh background, email4loveAsia.com.

Religion-Related Sites

Soulmatch.com. A branch of Beliefnet, a multifaith online community, Soulmatch is an attractive interfaith site founded in 2004 to help "people meet their spiritual needs," according to the mission statement. "Perhaps no spiritual need is greater than our need for companionship, connection, and love." Soulmatch provides a questionnaire that emphasizes values, personality, and faith. Members are asked to adhere to a code that prohibits hanky-panky, such as searching for romance if you're married, or posting inaccurate photos. You can do a free quick search based on personality and faith: Christian, Catholic, Mormon, Jewish, Muslim, Buddhist, Hindu, humanist, pagan, or other.

JDate.com. This hip site bills itself as "the largest Jewish singles network," with 500,000 members. JDate has many of the amenities you'd find on much bigger sites. Members can participate in travel (Hawaii, western Caribbean), poolside parties, Broadway outings, and volunteer work through the program "Hooking Up and Helping Out."

Orthodate.com. There's a certain charm to this low-key site for Orthodox Jews. "Your bashert could be just a click away," Orthodate promises. "We have about 3,000 members and several Shadchans who use our site for their clients," according to their very efficient help desk.

CatholicSingles.com. Founded in 1997, CatholicSingles.com promotes itself as "the largest Catholic singles site of its kind." Unique features include special events and trips, Catholic news, and advice from Catholic religious leaders.

BigChurch.com. This online community, an affiliate of the FriendFinder network, includes a 268,000-member dating section within the broader, million-member worldwide site. Members can search for Christian singles and participate in Bible study and prayer partnerships.

ChristianCafe.com. Although much smaller than BigChurch, ChristianCafe.com is solely focused on dating. Their motto: "All Christian. All Single."

LdsSingles.com. "Really big site. Really cool people." is the handle for the 200,000-member site for members of the Church of Jesus Christ of Latter-day Saints.

DharmaDate.com. Launched in February 2004, DharmaDate "aims to bring together Buddhist laypeople from around the world for friendship and marriage."

Zawaj.com. The Muslim religion forbids dating, but the site does encourage correspondence.

Weight-Related Sites

BBWPersonalsPlus.com is the most attractive of the sites for big, beautiful women and their admirers. There are also LargeFriends.com, LargeandLovely.com, and OverweightDate.com, which serve big beautiful women and big handsome men.

MAKING YOUR CHOICES

Which sites seem right for you? Take time to survey several—remember, the initial browse is free! As you shop, check first to see if it's easy for you to maneuver around a site. Is the technology user-friendly or intimidating? If you're not comfortable, you may avoid logging on and searching.

Next, consider the numbers. Does the initial browse turn up a good crop of candidates in your geographic area and age range? Do they seem appealing and match your interests? A free browse may not reveal all the criteria you pinpointed in chapter 2, but you should have a sense that the potential for a match could be there.

Finally, don't feel that you have to zero in on one site. Play the field. Monthly subscriptions cost about as much as dinner at a good restaurant. Try as many as your budget and time allow.

IN SIGHT FOR SITES

Sites constantly improve their services and technology. They also don't seem to mind "borrowing" good ideas from one another. I predict these changes in the very near future:

↑ **More consolidation.** The pet-lover category, for example, offers very little distinction among the competing sites. Bigger services will probably fold them into their databases, which will work to the user's advantage if the partnerships are well thought out, as happened in the case of Yahoo! Personals and ThirdAge Personals.

↑ **Trendier technology.** Match.com is pointing the way with the Physical Attraction Test, for example, which uses a cutting-edge recognition program. Some technology I'd rather not see adapted, however, like Mobile Match. This kind of rushed dating undermines the true strength of the online experience—getting to know someone in a measured way.

↑ **Consumer protection.** More sites will follow the lead of True.com and conduct felony and sexual-offense background searches on all members. Philanderers will be targeted, too—the technology to out the married is already available. I also suspect that there will soon be more regulation on how dating services conduct business.

↑ **Better guidance.** PerfectMatch.com is a model of how reassuring and effective at matching a site can be. The research, expertise, and hand-holding through the process set new standards that I hope other sites will try to emulate. ↖

As soon as you're set on your sites, we'll head into search. Get ready for some happy hunting!

RESOURCES

I selected sites that have staying power. New ones appear all the time, however. These online resources can keep you up to date:

↗ **Onlinedatingmagazine.com** offers news, short features, tips, and reviews of dating sites.

↗ **Edatereview.com** asks real people to write reviews. Categories include Top Rated, General Dating Sites, Free Personals, Christian Dating, Ethnic Dating, and more. ↖

THE SEARCH
IS ON

Now that you've done your spadework, you're ready for some online fun. Prepare to be flattered, amused, excited, and energized as you search in a strategic and dignified way. This chapter will cover the three ways to search and the three stages of search. I bet you'll soon have more suitors in one week than you've ever had in your lifetime. When my 58-year-old friend Hildy posted on two sites, she netted more than 235 e-mails overnight. That's not an atypical response to a well-worded, well-placed profile. This chapter will also show you how to keep up with such romantic riches.

SEARCH STRATEGY NO. 1:
The Passive Profile

If you followed the tips in chapters 4 and 5, you can sit back and relax. To paraphrase the movie *Field of Dreams*, "If you post it, they will come." (But if your profile generates a puny response, see "What, No E-Mail?" on the next page.)

Notice that I wrote "you *can* sit back and relax." That doesn't mean you have to. You may want to if you're superbusy or feel awkward about approaching a man. Let me try to talk you out of these excuses, though, because I think your chances will be better if you take an active role in the search.

"I'm too busy." In the introduction to this book, I made the case for marriage. A quick recap: A good marriage is one of the best ways to secure your health, happiness, and financial well-being. I have friends

WHAT, NO E-MAIL?

If your search is not generating results, it's not you. It's probably your standards or your profile. Open up your geographic range, for starters. I thought I was a committed city woman, a real Manhattanite. Yet as I write, I'm looking out at the green grass and trees of suburban New Jersey. Love can change your mind and location. Expand your search to a hundred-mile radius, or be daring and look anywhere and everywhere, literally around the world.

Reexamine the physical requirements you checked in your questionnaire. Does one less inch of height matter that much? Be generous on the first round of search, and cull later.

Review the tips in the previous chapters for creating your profile and questionnaire. Look especially closely for evidence of male bashing. I wondered why the in-box was empty for 49-year-old Carol, a real-estate professional with beautiful auburn hair and green eyes. Then I saw her profile headline: "Looking for a NORMAL, not boring guy! Are you out there?" Here are some other mistakes she made:

"Life is too short to spend it alone. Although I am always busy, I'd like to find someone who shares my interests, would like to travel, and eventually perhaps find someone to share the rest of my life with." Do not announce loneliness. Do not ask for a lifetime commitment.

"I have met my share of odd dating characters in the past few years. It's time to find someone normal. Are you normal? Normal but not boring? Interesting but not overwhelming?" Carol doesn't realize how insulting these questions are. She's also painting a picture of herself as a magnet for maniacs. This is a far cry from the successful, dynamic, amusing woman she truly is.

Ask a friend for an objective evaluation of your profile and photo. What needs changing? Remember, every time you revise or update your profile, it's as if you were a new subscriber. The profile moves to the front of the site. ➤

and family members who lead well-rounded, enjoyable lives as single women and men. I had an interesting, fun-filled single life myself. But being married (happily, that is) is better. If you didn't believe that, too, I doubt you would have purchased this book.

So it comes down to priorities. You can use your free time to watch *The Bachelor* on TV, or search and find your own real-life bachelor. Even if you are a single, harried, working mom, as I was, there's an hour somewhere in your day or evening to hit the computer.

"I feel awkward about approaching men." I come from a Deep South family of five daughters. My mother raised us with traditional values about the sexes. My friend Jan Harayda still remembers my mother's pronouncement of 30 years ago: "If I caught one of my girls calling up a man, well, I think I'd cut her finger off!"

Perhaps you were brought up as conservatively as I was. You still hesitate to approach the opposite sex because that's not how you were taught to behave. The good news about being older is that you're not a kid anymore. You can make your own rules for the adult you. Even my mother has changed—slightly—with the times.

Also remember, the men who have taken the time to post their profiles *expect* and *want* to hear from women. If you walked into a bar, you wouldn't know a guy's intention. He might be there to meet a friend or to relax after a long day. A man online couldn't be clearer: *I am here on this site for singles because I want to find a relationship. I want you to contact me.*

You will do fine, even fabulously, if you post your profile and wait for the crowd to come to you. But you may miss some fabulous prospects.

SEARCH STRATEGY NO. 2:
The Computer Knows Best

I'm a believer in the wisdom of the computer. When I signed up with Matchmaker.com and completed the questionnaire, I was asked if I wanted the computer to make me a match. The computer's choices for me were ranked on a compatibility scale. I read the profile of its number one choice. Not only did Number One meet my standard criteria, his essay pointed to subtle signs that he could be soul-mate material. We celebrated our four-year wedding anniversary in January.

Many other sites, including PerfectMatch.com and Match.com, also claim to have compatibility down to a science. Take a chance on an electronic fix-up. It was right on the money for me.

SEARCH STRATEGY NO. 3:
Don't Just Sit There—Do Something

There could be several reasons a likely candidate hasn't contacted you. He could be too busy to search regularly. He also could be a passive profiler: perhaps he's sensitive about being bald or a little overweight and only wants to contact women who first demonstrate an interest in him. Or he may not be as discerning as you are, so he skipped you inadvertently.

Feel confident that you've done a thorough job of finding the best man and be an active player in creating your own love life. Contact anyone who looks interesting.

Optimize your opportunities. Use all three strategies.

ABOUT FACE (AND BODY)

Are you too judgmental about looks? Do you get stuck on a physical type and make the same mistakes with the same kind of people over and over again? Try a computer-generated match. The computer is objective. It searches for a psychological/social fit that's more likely to guarantee commitment and contentment. Maybe the computer's match for you is someone who is shorter than you generally like or a bit older-looking. See if the positive personality factors override a minor physical trait. ↖

THE STAGES OF SEARCH

When my husband and I take our boat and trawl net out into the Gulf of Mexico, we're never quite sure what we'll gather for dinner. As we empty the bag, we quickly toss overboard the sweet but too tiny crabs and flounder, along with the nastier creatures like stingrays and jellyfish. The big catch becomes smaller, more manageable—the perfect size. With a bit of organization and sensible selecting, it's easy to winnow prospects to a good number.

Stage-One Search: The Early Eliminations

One of the strengths of Internet dating is that it's anonymously impersonal, which helps take the sting out of rejection. If you're interested in someone who notices your profile or you're intrigued by a computer-generated match, let the e-mail begin. If you're not interested, delete the e-mail with about the same level of remorse you'd feel from dumping jellyfish overboard. Unnecessary politeness with the wrong catch wastes your time. Do you feel obliged to read every pop-up add on your computer? The same thinking applies here. Eliminate time wasters right away. And for safety reasons, delete sketchy types as well. For example:

Form letters. If someone sends a canned reply, he's either too cold, too busy, or too much of a player for a real relationship.

Sexy handles. Could you really keep a straight face if you met someone who called himself LoverMan or Adonis? Any sexy reference in an initial e-mail is totally inappropriate.

Negative attitude toward women. *His ex is out to get him. He's tired of women who only want a free meal ticket. He hates women who try to tell him how to live.* Even if you are the ideal woman, it's only a matter of time before this kind of guy turns on you, too.

Universally hostile or supersecretive. This fellow isn't only hostile to women. He's a bundle of anger who blames everyone else for his problems. Does he claim to work for a top-secret organization like the CIA? He's too spooky for you.

Too perfect. Experts on Internet safety say that someone who sounds too good to be true may be bad news. Avoid people who hyperbolize about fantastic wealth, charm, and prowess.

Overly enthusiastic e-mail. Is his ardor over-the-top right from the start? It could be a sign that he's extremely jealous, controlling, a sexual predator, or just not cool.

Profiles without a photo. Chances are he's either married, or older or less attractive than he says.

Poor spelling and grammar. These can be a tip-off to education or merely indicate a man in a hurry.

EXCEPTION TO THE RULES

Forty-year-old Sandy Klein of Bend, Oregon, took a chance on Greg Thoma's profile in Yahoo! Personals. "He had so much wrong," she says. "He couldn't spell. His grammar was terrible. He didn't have a photo up. Yet there was something I just kept coming back to. I had this gut feeling about him because we had so many interests in common. We both even had cats named Fred. But the clincher was that he wrote 'love to laugh' not once but twice in the profile. I really wanted that."

They arranged to meet for lunch and were instantly attracted. "We had so much fun talking," she says, "we never dated anyone after that."

Three years after that first meeting Sandy and Greg were married in the community theater his mother owns and manages. They took advantage of the venue to stage their wedding in two acts. In Act I they reenacted a funny take on how they met online. Act II was the traditional ceremony.

"I tell people I found a husband who's part Labrador retriever," says Sandy. "He's the friendliest, most easygoing and affectionate person ever. We work together now and enjoy every minute of the day with each other."

"I don't think you have enough life experience to pick a soul mate until you get a bit older," adds Greg. "Young guys want bling bling—the hottest new thing out there. But Sandy . . . Sandy just butters my heart up." ✒

Wrong age. The rule of thumb among most dating experts is to keep the boundaries within 10 years of your age, older and younger, to avoid a generation gap.

Also use your intuition and avoid e-mails and profiles that don't make sense or leave you feeing uncomfortable in any way (see chapter 9 for more on these). No answer may be the perfect answer to all of the above.

Stage-Two Search: Courtship Contenders

Once you've made the easy eliminations, take a closer look at the Courtship Contenders. These are the men who deserve your time and attention—for a while, anyway. You don't want to miss that diamond in the rough.

Your preliminary search also will open your eyes to what you value. With each decision you make, you'll come closer to knowing what your ideal is.

When I went out with Courtship Contender Steven, for example, I was crazy about his outgoing personality. He kept me laughing. He charmed my friends. We had so much fun. But there was something about the way he treated waiters and taxi drivers that bothered me. I worried that he might get snappish with me, and one day he did. I found out I liked an outgoing type but needed unqualified niceness, too.

Robert was as courteous as he was romantic. He crooned to me in his beautiful baritone as we danced on New Year's Eve. He showed up with thoughtful presents, sent sweet and funny cards, never failed to call. But there was something about the way he let his career slide that I didn't respect. I found out I liked romance but needed an achieving attitude, too.

Phil was successful and good-looking, truly dashing in the exquisite pastel cashmere sweaters he wore. I enjoyed driving with him on snowy evenings. He made sure the seat warmer in his luxury SUV kept me snug and cozy until we reached one of his finds—a romantic gourmet restaurant in the country. He impressed me with his knowledge of fine wines, and the restaurant staff made a fuss over him. He tipped handsomely so we were seated at the best table near the fireplace. But there was something about his stiffness that chilled me. I found out I could really get used to the good life but needed genuine warmth, too.

Then there was Mario—a second-generation American with deep Italian roots. He was warm and affable, and it was interesting to be with someone from such a different background than mine. He treated me to his mother's homemade pasta and fresh tomato sauce. I was entertained by the stories of his childhood and family life. But there was something about the way he spent *every* summer weekend at his family's estate on Long Island that bothered me. I found out I liked men with roots and family but preferred roots that I could identify with and a family in which I could be included.

When I met Walter, I knew I'd found the complete package—outgoing, courteous, romantic, successful, warm, close to his family but open to me. Would I have fallen for him so surely and easily without the advanced preparation from the other guys? Oh, yeah. But I wouldn't have appreciated him nearly as much.

Only you will know when it's time to cut bait with a second-stage prospect. You may not like the tone of an e-mail. He may be pressuring you to meet him, and you're not ready. There may be nonnegotiable problems when you do meet. Be as objective as you can for as long as you can, and then move on with a quick and kind goodbye (see chapter 8).

Stage-Three Search: Selecting a Soul Mate

You know the saying "opposites attract." You've heard stories and jokes about May-December romances. The reason people tend to talk and tease about these kinds of relationships is that they are *not* the norm. In actuality, the most apt adage would be "birds of a feather flock together." For example:

- Ninety-four percent of all marriages are racially and ethnically homogenous.

- Partners from different socioeconomic, ethnic, and cultural backgrounds traditionally have a higher divorce rate.
- Nearly half of married couples involve two people with the same level of education.
- Most husbands and wives are of similar age, with husbands an average of three years older.

Online dating selects for the common bonds that create rapport and goes one step further. Not only can you seek someone close in age, education, and background, you can look for multiple points of connection. For example: similar personality traits, shared habits, parallel interests, common values, and joint leisure activities. These are also key factors that predict marital stability, according to a study by sociologist Martin Whyte.

The computer opens up the field so that you can have incredible access to candidates who share many of your core interests and your outlook on life. With a click, you can investigate remote possibilities or someone living practically next door. But without the Internet, your wires would never cross.

"Michael and I lived forty-five minutes away from each other, but we never would have met," says 42-year-old Pam Pierre of Middletown, Ohio. "It was awesome the way the personals linked two people with so much in common. He even likes dirt-track racing. I told myself, 'Finally, someone who likes to play in the dirt, too.'"

A month after meeting on Yahoo! Personals, the couple went to a wedding together. Michael leaned over and whispered in her ear, "One of these days you'll walk down the aisle with me." Eleven months later she did.

Now married a little over a year, Pam says they haven't had even minor ups and downs. "Michael works with me. He wants to succeed the same way I do, and I've accomplished more and do more than I ever have before. I was not a camper, but he converted me. I talked him into joining a gym with me. He brings out my happiness."

Pam feels she learned from her first marriage and doesn't want to repeat those mistakes with Michael. "Once you've had a bad divorce," she says, "you don't ever want to go back there. Michael and I say 'I love you' to each other about thirty times a day, and not in a casual way. I look him straight in the eye. I want him to feel that I mean it."

Review your Must List on page 46. It may be a good idea to keep it by your computer to refresh your memory while you search. Continue to ask yourself, "What all do I need?" In a January 2004 survey commissioned by Match.com, "quality of character" followed by "sense of humor" were the key traits that led to love, according to online daters who later married. What character traits are on your list? Also remember the desires on your list—the fun stuff. In that same Match.com survey, marriage partners said that they also selected each other because of similar or complementary leisure and work pursuits.

In short, you can find all that you want, more than you expect. He's out there—the man that Pam says will fit you "like a key in a lock." The next chapter tells how to create e-mail magic with your best prospects, but first, here are some ways to organize your guys.

ORGANIZATION MAKES YOUR SEARCH EASIER

When your search and e-mailing get active, you'll need a way to keep up with who's who. (Trust me, if your memory is like mine, you'll need an aid. Nothing is as embarrassing or as insulting as confusing your

THE LONGEST MILE

Brian and his fiancée, Pam, were a near miss. They had attended the same 1,200-student college and had never met. The same church and had never met. They had the same doctor and never met. When eHarmony united the couple, it was easy to plan a first date. Pam drove the 5,280 feet to Brian's driveway, then they went bowling. ➤

correspondents.) Some sites help with the organizational chores by keeping track of your searches. If they don't, use spreadsheet programs, such as Excel, or contact managers like Act to note the details. Or simply write one name per page in a loose-leaf notebook.

Another suggestion: Store e-mails in folders on your computer. This saves time with future correspondence. You can cut and paste his remarks into your e-mails without retyping long passages—"Remember when you wrote . . . " An e-mail archive is also a good refresher before that first meeting. As you review your messages to each other, you'll find topics ready to discuss.

The best reason of all to save your journal notes and e-mails is that they may become treasured mementos. I wish I had been wise enough to save all my husband's e-mails. But I did save this one, which he sent the morning after our first meeting. We printed it on the back of our wedding program.

Judsen,

I wish I had made plans to stay out later, as I was having such a good time. Hope I didn't talk too much, but when I meet someone who lights me up like you did (which happens very infrequently, I might add) I can't seem to shut up.

Have a great weekend. Hope you can get some golf in. I'll call you when I get back from Charlotte on Wednesday. Maybe you'd like to come out here next Saturday or Sunday for a round of golf with me. I'll call.

Walter

PART

Three

CREATING CONNECTION

HOW TO USE THE MAGIC OF
E-MAIL TO ENCHANT SOMEONE

EVERYTHING YOU NEED TO
KNOW TO STAY SAFE

HOW TO PREPARE FOR YOUR
FIRST MEETING

LESSONS IN FLIRTATION

E-MAIL MAGIC

Every night during the summer of 2001, as soon as the kitchen was cleaned up and her 11- and 12-year-old sons were settled down, Charlene Black of Greenwood, South Carolina, would head for the computer. This was *her* time—her time to court and spark in cyberspace.

Charlene corresponded with a man she met on Yahoo! Personals. Steve was from her old hometown, so there was a sense of familiarity right from the start. They also shared a desire to try new things, a "let's-get-up-and-go spirit," as Charlene calls it. For three months they traded e-mails without even a phone conversation.

"I was patient," she says. "I didn't give out too much information right away. I just kept reading and writing e-mails to give a chance to someone who sounded like what I wanted."

Their initial phone call lasted more than an hour. After a month of calls that got progressively longer, they decided, a little nervously, to meet.

"We had no problem talking at that first meeting," she says. "It felt right being with him because we figured out so much in e-mails. I tell people now, 'There's a soul mate for you out there somewhere. Don't settle. Find the person who treats you like gold, just like my husband treats me.'"

A FAVORITE WAY TO COMMUNICATE

Charlene's story illustrates why e-mailing your way into a relationship is so popular. First, e-mail is easy to control. You choose when to interact:

first thing in the morning, a fast little check-in on your lunch break, or after you've had a chance to unwind at night. E-mail waits respectfully for you. It will not intrude on your time and mood with a ring, beep, blink, or buzz like a phone, cell phone, answering machine, or pager.

Second, e-mail makes correspondence easy. It's simpler to correct than a handwritten or typed letter, and more informal. Simpler to send, too—one click and it's off.

Another plus is that guys especially like the medium. I remember a day when my son and a buddy sat side by side with laptops. I peeked at a screen and saw that they were in e-mail chat with each other. When I pointed out that it might be easier to, well, just plain talk, they glanced up for a split second to deliver a withering, adolescent look that said "You're so out of it."

The Internet's appeal seems to grow stronger as men age. A report from Media Metrix shows that 45- to 64-year-olds surf the Internet more frequently, stay logged on 236 minutes longer, and view 179 more unique pages per month than 18- to 24-year-olds do. Match.com found that the ratio of men to women on Internet dating sites is 60/40. More evidence of male interest comes from a telephone survey conducted in 2000 for FriendFinder.com, which revealed that men are three times more likely than women to have tried to find a romantic interest online.

Social scientists who study computer-mediated communication (CMC) have looked at a number of reasons, besides convenience and ease, for the popularity of e-mail–based courtship. Their findings offer some interesting insights that seem particularly helpful in understanding the dynamics of online relationships in general, as well as the specific attraction they hold for male e-mailers. Why, for example, do men seem to be so much more open when they're online?

Hello, Stranger

The anonymity of online dating has distinct social and emotional advantages over other types of interactions, including face-to-face meetings. If, for example, John Smith introduced himself to you at a bar, he probably would not get around to talking about his love of Italian arias, bone fishing, and Patrick O'Brien novels. Men are not as forthcoming about these kinds of personal details as women are. However, these more multifaceted aspects of John would be instantly knowable upon reading his online profile and questionnaire. An e-mail correspondence would further break the ice, adding more clues about his personality, feelings, and interests.

The Internet "enables partners to get past the usual obstacles or 'gates' that in traditional interaction settings often prevent potentially rewarding relationships from getting off the ground," according to researchers at New York University who have studied Internet dating.

A gate might be the limitations of the meeting place, such as a bar or noisy party. A gate can also be psychological, such as feeling shy, socially anxious, or concerned about appearance. In studies, computer users say they don't feel as self-conscious online as they would being ogled and evaluated in person. This comfort level lays the foundation for the Cycle of Rapport.

The Cycle of Rapport

It takes courage to disclose the inner self. In most everyday situations, we don't want neighbors, colleagues, and acquaintances to know "all our business," as the saying goes. Usually we're so wary of baring our souls that we save our deepest truths for our most significant long-term relationships. Even this is risky.

Although you may trust family and friends in many, many ways, part of you may also fear their ridicule or rejection—with good reason. They may be loving but not objective. They may be too invested in your past and think they know you too well to consider a new dimension to your interests and dreams. They may fear losing what was once true about you to what you may want to become.

Imagine if John let it slip to his pals that he was enthralled with

Puccini. His best buddy might remark disapprovingly, "What's with you and this opera stuff? Hey, Frank, check this out, John's getting real fancy on us. I guess rock and roll isn't good enough for him now."

Sharing secrets with a less restrictive, more accepting e-mail correspondent—especially if you're a guy—may seem safer and more liberating in comparison. Indeed, online communication sets up a sequence of reflection, revelation, and connection that creates a kind of magic and builds remarkable rapport.

Reflection. Composing a profile or e-mail forces you to pause and think positively about what psychologist Carl Rogers termed "the true self." The true self is the inner person that you believe yourself to be—not, say, the macho role guys slip into when out with the boys, or the good little girl women tend to revert to when around relatives. It feels emotionally satisfying and freeing to spend time exploring the real you, calling forth all your complexity—the tender side as well as your feistiness.

The process of writing deepens introspection and increases self-understanding and self-liking in a way that may not be possible anywhere else in your life, according to online psychiatrist Esther Gwinnell, M.D., in her book *Online Seductions*. No one sees, hears, or judges you as you write in private, so you can be more open and experiment with offering up different aspects of your personality.

Men, in particular, often have even fewer opportunities to scratch below the surface, so self-reflection may feel especially liberating and pleasurable to them. And as they search their hearts, thoughts about love may rise to a conscious level.

Revelation. Naturally, if a guy's aglow with self-discovery, he wants to share those positive feelings with an accepting audience: for example, someone who sends an e-mail that indicates she liked the "real me" presented in his profile. The recognition plants the first seeds of trust. He then feels safe revealing to an empathetic admirer even more of his interests, emotions, and beliefs.

When social scientists conducted the first CMC studies, they were surprised to find that many online correspondents have deeper, more intimate levels of disclosure than daters who've only talked face-to-face. Ironically, cool, impersonal technology creates a platform for warm, personal communication.

Connection. Each e-mail is a new opportunity to reinforce the intimate process. As a bond builds, it stimulates even more reflection and revelation, which leads to deeper connection, the Cycle of Rapport churning repeatedly. Love has an excellent chance to develop—and develop quickly—when two people find the match for the true self and set off the Cycle.

The power of online communication, however, is not a cue to rush into information overload. Clearly, there are many reasons to be careful and cool about what you say to an Internet acquaintance (see chapter 9). Love also needs space for mystery, infatuation, and a bit of a chase. As tempting as it is to share your soul right way, you need to dance between distance and intimacy.

PACE YOURSELF

There's a rhythm to romance online. Studies of online relationships by Anita Baker, Ph.D., of Ohio University, suggest that three months is the optimal period to get to know someone through their e-mails before talking by phone or meeting. That seems like an awfully long stretch, especially if you're very interested in someone. But consider this: once you break out of the magical space of e-mail communication, it will be almost impossible to put that genie back in the bottle. You will gain all the richness of face-to-face communication, but you will lose some of the intimacy and power of e-mail: the self-reflection, the creativity, the self-disclosure, and the sharing that can take place when you're relaxed and without distractions. I still look back fondly on my six-week e-mail courtship with Walter. I wouldn't have shortchanged it for the world.

Yet there are several good reasons to go face-to-face sooner than six weeks to three months. Your dating skills may be rusty, and you may not know what you want from a relationship. If that's true, do set up training dates with Courtship Contenders. These practice runs will sharpen your behavior and thinking.

Or perhaps you're at an impasse with a Contender. You're not sure he's Soul Mate class, but you're not ready to pass on him, either. An in-person meeting may be the only way to make a decision. It could save you from wasting time on more e-mails.

Another reason to break off sooner than six weeks is that e-mail may not be your medium: typing—even with voice-recognition software—bothers you, or you may be strong in oral skills, weak in writing. But do give e-mailing a good try. Half of Yahoo! Personals subscribers had at least 10 e-mail exchanges before meeting. Chances are you, too, will

QUICK AND KIND GOODBYES

There's an unwritten rule that e-mails should be exchanged on a one-to-one basis, according to computer-mediated communication researchers. If an e-mail is not responded to after a reasonable time, it's customary to interpret this as a signal of disinterest. Expect that half the men you contact may not get back to you. But it works both ways. You don't have to reply to all the men who contact you. Even if you initially reply and then decide a candidate is not for you, it's okay to do nothing and let things lapse. His contact may be flattering, but so is a whistle from a passing driver. This is not a relationship yet. It's just a scouting report. There are also important safety considerations that justify ignoring Early Eliminations (see chapter 9).

But let's say you've had reciprocal e-mail exchanges, perhaps five or more. Then you uncover a fatal flaw—he's a confirmed night owl, for example, while you're a morning person. You can still take the lapse approach. He will soon tire of no answer and move on. Some online relationship advisors would say this is cold or bad manners. After all, he's invested time in you. I disagree. To me, lapsing is like a no-fault divorce, an easier and less emotional way to get out of a wrong relationship. (Remember this, and don't feel hurt, if an e-mailer simply disappears on you.)

become better at creating messages and will find it more enjoyable. If not, keep the text short, and switch to telephone communication or a meeting as soon as you're ready.

Pacing Pointers

Be approachable but cool on first contact. *If you initiated a search* that uncovers a likely candidate, you may want to send an initial e-mail that's as short and simple as "I like your profile. Want to take a look at mine?" For a stronger possibility, offer more: "You sound like someone who really likes golf. I'm an 18 handicap myself. (Or, "You sound interesting/amusing/delightful.") Would you like to peek at my profile?"

I do think serious correspondence—10 e-mails or more—deserves a response. Here are dos and don'ts for a better online breakup:

↑ **Do** remember why you're using online dating services. Your goal is to find a match, not a pen pal. If relationship potential is not there, you are doing both of you a favor to stop corresponding and look for someone more suited.

↑ **Don't** feel guilty about leading someone on. Everyone online is in an experimental mode. It may take a lot of information, and many e-mails, to reach a conclusion. The process itself is a valuable learning experience.

↑ **Don't** justify your decision. Any reason you give may trigger a war of words in which he tries to overcome your objections.

↑ **Do** be short, definite, and emotionally neutral. Avoid offering friendship or excessive apologies. A perfect response might be something like: "I've had some time to reflect, and this is not working for me. Good luck in your search!"

↑ **Do** stick to your guns. As child psychologists say, "No is an answer." Anyone with high self-esteem will respect your decision. ↖

If it's *someone who noticed your profile and contacted you*, review his profile before you answer. Remember, you do not have to respond to Early Eliminations (see chapter 7 and "Quick and Kind Goodbyes" on page 126). If he's a Courtship Contender, be polite and curious. That first impression counts.

Hello Steve,

Thanks for writing me. We do seem to have a number of interests in common. I'd like to know more about you.

If it's a *computer-generated match*, you have a prequalified prospect. Handle with more warmth and TLC. My first e-mail to Walter went something like this:

Hey, Walter,

Guess what? You're my #1 match on Matchmaker.com. When I browsed your profile, it looked as if we do have quite a lot in common. I spent some of my childhood in North Carolina, for example, and have great memories of the state. Go TARHEELS! I'd enjoy knowing more about a Southerner living in Northern New Jersey. Why not take a look at my profile.

Slow and steady wins the date. Don't be in a rush after the initial contact. Wait a day before replying. Give yourself a chance to think about what you want to say. Intrigue him by being coy. A good rule of thumb is to stay a couple of clicks behind him. An eager e-mailer may send you one or two missives a day. Respond once every day or two. A more typical schedule from him would be a few e-mails a week. Stay slightly behind that schedule. A very busy guy may pop up once a week or disappear for long stretches. Wait him out if he seems like a catch, but look for hints that he's preoccupied . . . with a wife, for example, or a string of women.

Disclose gradually. Online correspondence is storytelling: the story of you; the story of him. Don't rush to the conclusion. Allow the characters to unfold in stages. Best-selling mystery writer Kate White never divulges too many clues in the opening chapters of her Bailey Weggins novels. Keep your reader in such tantalizing suspense.

The first couple of weeks, you may want to confine the topics of your correspondence to interests and activities. Ask clarifying, open-ended questions and extend his thoughts. ("I've hiked trails in the Adirondacks about a dozen times, but I've never thought about trying a birding trail. Tell me more. How did you get started?")

AVOID THE R-WORD

It's mighty tempting to ask and tell about relationship histories. You can fill e-mail after e-mail with empathetic exchanges. I had one cyber-pal whose outrageous ex kept me glued to the computer as though I were reading one of Dorothea Benton Frank's novels. What would that woman be up to next? You can see the problem with this. He and I were so focused on the old, other relationship that it overwhelmed anything that we could get going. When I tired of the role of therapist and voyeur, we had little common ground.

There will come a time when you move into very serious stages of courtship. Then you will want to reveal something you've learned from the past: how to communicate better, for example. In the e-mailing stages, however, say as little as possible, and say it neutrally: "My ex and I are on good terms now."

Beware, too, of people who try to coerce you into true confessions. On her first date with an e-acquaintance, my friend Hildy felt badgered into talking about the past. The next day, the very same man who extracted her emotional response e-mailed to say that she needed time to recover from old wounds.

If bringing up the R-word in terms of the past is bad, using it in a future context may be worse. Avoid mentioning *relationship*, *commitment*, and *long-term plans* in your e-mails, the same way you avoid these loaded words in your profile. Have you, for example, ever called to get a quote on car insurance only to be bombarded with a sales pitch for a long-term care policy? It's off-putting, right? You may even need the long-term care policy, but not now and not from this antsy agent. The same principle applies. Your goal is to get a date. Period. Everlasting love needs time and trust to develop. You should not lay out that expectation in an early e-mail.

As you create trust and connection through your shared interests, expand your queries in a more personal direction. The questions that follow may help trigger some revealing writing. Enjoy the magic!

The Art of Questioning

Questions are a perfect way to keep correspondence lively as you discover more about your compatibility. It's tempting, of course, to try to get all your questions answered at once. Tempting, but wrong. My friend Marion blew off one e-mailer because his questions were more like an interrogation from a prosecutor. Keep it to a couple of queries per e-mail. And, as with the rest of your search and correspondence, start lightly and work in stages.

Stage-One Questions

A Courtship Contender's profile and questionnaire may have addressed many of the nonnegotiable items on your Must List. You may already know, for example, that he's a nonsmoker who has older children, an income, and a geographically feasible address. Try a few questions to get a better sense of him: "How much time do you spend on favorite activities?" "When did you learn how to salsa?" "Tell me about your favorite restaurants." "What kind of museums do you like?" "What are some of the things you could talk about forever?" At this stage, avoid asking any questions about relationships, commitment, or sex.

Stage-Two Questions

If you have a strong candidate among your Courtship Contenders, probe more deeply. Try to get to some items on your Must List: "What made you happy growing up?" "What's a typical day like for you?" "How would friends describe you?" "Why did you decide on a career in otolaryngology?" In addition, you may have special compatibility needs. Now is the time to discover how your Courtship Contender feels about vegetarianism, evangelism, extreme sports, or radical politics, for example.

Stage-Three Questions

You're beginning to think he has Soul Mate potential. Before you plunge into deeper territory, however, you want to be sure your important criteria are addressed. *How*, *why*, and *what* questions stimulate responses: "How do you try to stay healthy?" "How do you deal with stress?" "Why did you move to Santa Fe?" "What are your favorite memories of growing up in South Dakota?" "What would you like to be doing ten years from now?" His answers should tell you a lot about his personality, choices, and values.

THE FUNDAMENTALS OF E-MAIL

Creating a bond takes time. In the beginning especially, you want your online correspondence to be light, curious, and charming, a slow build to the Cycle of Rapport. Six rules to remember:

Happy is better than heavy. Cyberspace is not the place to air your relationship grievances or whine about your life. Stick to topics that reflect your positive interests, and leave downbeat discussions about your feelings for future meetings (very far in the future).

Flirtatious is better than sexy. Flirting means taking notice, showing interest, and offering reassurance. At its best it's a kind of flattery with genuine warmth. Be sure to browse carefully through his profile and questionnaire so that you can refer to his interests. Using his name is also a flirtatious personalization technique. ("John, what's your favorite thing to do on Martha's Vineyard? Is it a great place to take your mountain bike?") Outright sexiness, on the other hand, can be dangerous and a turnoff. Couples who engage in cybersex ("hot chat") break off their online relationships more frequently than abstinent e-mailers do, according to a study by Dr. Baker.

Colorful is better than quiet. Use descriptive language that reflects your personality and suggests vitality, good humor, and playfulness. Offer details that demonstrate you're fun and interesting to be with.

Warmth is better than sarcasm. You may think sarcasm demonstrates your funny side, but it doesn't play well in e-mail. It erodes the trust that is so necessary to self-disclosure. Without being able to see that twinkle in your eye, your correspondent might misunderstand you and think you have a mean streak. (Emoticons such as smiley faces ☺ don't offset a faintly hostile remark.) And men over age 40 are particularly unresponsive to a snippy, rejecting tone.

"Mature men are more likely to describe what they want from a woman in terms of 'warmth' and 'caring,'" says Stanley Woll, Ph.D., a professor of psychology at California State University who has studied dating services and personal ads for more than 20 years. "Younger men respond to the physical, but the psychological is much more important with the older."

Present is better than future. Whoa! He doesn't need to know what you expect from a future mate. Do not list your criteria for a husband. Do not even put the word *husband* in e-mails. As my friend David Barklow puts it, "Don't scare a man out of the corral before you can get the saddle on him for a first date." Stick to the here and now. (See "Avoid The R-Word" on page 129.)

Good grammar is better than bad grammar. As noted in chapter 7, there are exceptions to this rule, especially if you happen to be online with someone from a specific-interest site where colloquial writing is the norm. But, in general, most e-mailers get annoyed with sloppy grammar. Bad spelling also grates, although a bit of e-mailese can be fun ("huggs," "newz"). The latest e-mail software offers a fast and easy way to check grammar and spelling. Take advantage of this one-click editing feature. (You can also work in a word-processing program, like Word, that has a spell-check button, and cut and paste your compositions into an e-mail.) Other bothersome no-nos that may generate deletes: USE OF CAPITALS THROUGHOUT AN E-MAIL, which connotes shouting or hyperactivity; long, disorganized monologues; overuse of exclamatory punctuation; and irritating instant messages.

EMOTICONS AND NARRATIVE ASIDES

Because e-mailing misses the visual and auditory cues of face-to-face meetings, e-mailers have invented a creative emotional shorthand. But emoticons, narrative asides, and other keyboarding tricks are not a substitute for clear writing. "Good writing and expressiveness are still the best ways to make a point, whether serious, sarcastic, or silly," says Joseph Walther, Ph.D., professor of computer-mediated communication at Cornell University. "Emoticons," according to his research, "have little impact on the actual message." But these expressive strategies, which originated in chat rooms, can add spice when lightly peppered into your correspondence.

Emoticons	Meanings
:-(	frowning
:-/	frustrated
:-D	grinning
{ }	hug
:-*)	kiss
:-)	smiling
:-}	wry smile
:-p	sticking one's tongue out
:-O	surprised
;-)	winking

Narrative Asides	Meanings
BRB	be right back
F2F	face-to-face
GMTA	great minds think alike
GTG	got to go
IMHO	in my humble opinion
LOL	laughing out loud
OIC	oh, I see
PLS	please
ROFL	rolling on the floor laughing
SO	significant other

Elements of E-Mail Style

Even someone who's rusty at putting pen to paper may find composing an e-mail creatively satisfying, like keeping a journal or diary. E-mail satisfies the sender's need to be creative and self-revealing, to spend quality time with the self in an engaging activity. And it meets the receiver's need to be noticed, chosen, and connected.

"An e-mail message is a tiny packet of self-representation," writes John Suler, Ph.D., of Rider University. It's a "creative work, a gift sent to one's Internet pal. It's a piece of oneself that experienced e-mail users enjoy constructing." Here, from his online book, *The Psychology of Cyberspace*, are Dr. Suler's tips to make e-mails richer and more expressive:

Make the subject line snappier. Are you wasting this space with a dull summary? Instead, use it to tease and pique interest in your message. For example:

The solution is . . .

Jim! help, Help, HELP! (Note the clever, not excessive, use of caps.)

Loved it!

Thanks for your compliment and support, really!

Sigh . . .

Change the subject line. Hitting reply and reusing the same subject line over and over (with an ever-lengthening string of RE:s) make the correspondence feel stale. Freshen up with a new topic heading, such as:

And now for something completely different

Are you ready for this?

NEWZ!

Go with a great greeting. "Dear" doesn't do it for e-mailers. It smacks of snail mail. Try these as your relationship progresses:

Hello Steve or *Hello, Steve* is a good first-time greeting. It's friendly and casual, "with a hint of politeness and respect," says Dr. Suler. A plain *Hello* without a name is too impersonal.

Hi Steve works for a third or fourth e-mail. It shows the relationship is heading for friendlier footing.

Hi Steve! or *Steve!!!* conveys enthusiasm. Use exclamation points to highlight exciting news or emotion, but steer away from overuse.

Add some color. An entire e-mail written in the color lavender or with a lavender background is as annoying and hard to read as is all caps all the time. But a judicious jolt of color can be playful and expressive. Use a background color to emphasize a sentence or paragraph. Type the word *angry* in red or *jubilation* in a rainbow of colors, suggests Dr. Suler. **Boldface**, *italics*, a new font, or different type size creates visual interest that shows a reader you've taken the time to craft a message. But be sparing. A light, sensitive hand is best, according to Dr. Suler.

Be creative with keyboarding. Use these simple tricks to convey warmth and humor.

Parentheses	That's such good news! (VERY good news!)
Brackets	I'm so proud of you [Wow!] or [[[HUGS]]]
Asterisks	I want to know what *you* think.
	I don't **think** so.
Ellipses	Well, . . . uh . . . that's an interesting question.
Caps	YES, of course.
Repetition	Happy birthday to yooooooouuuuuu!
	(happy, happy, happy)

End with a kicker. *Sincerely* and *Regards* are in the same category as *Dear*—stiff and postal. These more formal words may work well if you're trying to ease out of an e-mail correspondence. If you want to keep the lines of communication going, however, try these warmer, livelier endings:

Thanks for listening

Take good care

Heading to the gym . . .

Hit 'em straight!

Enjoy dinner with the boss (LOL)

HUGZZ

Before you know it, you'll really be enjoying your e-mail correspondence. You'll look forward to the messages waiting for you each day from your cyber-suitors, and as you post replies, the writing will become easier, even entertaining. The best part of all—e-mail magic will give you a proper and powerful introduction to the good guys you're about to meet. But first, a few cautions about not-so-good guys.

9

SAFETY CONCERNS

HOW TO AVOID THOSE LIARS, CADS, STALKERS, CHEATS, AND BOUNDERS

Every month an estimated 37 to 40 million people go online to meet others. With a number so huge, there *will* be bad guys in the bunch— but not nearly as many as sensational headlines may have led you to believe. Don't let misconceptions scare you out of your best chance to meet someone just right for you.

To begin, it's the exceptional incident that makes the news. The unusual, the spectacular, and the gruesome generate newsprint. Will you ever see a story: "50,000 Online Daters Found Someone They Liked This Week"? I don't think you will. The news is not skewed to our normal, everyday lives.

Then there's the misunderstanding that arises from the title confusion between Internet dating sites and Internet chat rooms. They share a similar name but are, in general, quite different. Chat rooms, for example, are free, and they do not require you to write a profile, post a photo, or complete a questionnaire. The ease of access means very limited natural screening takes place. There are no barriers to anyone joining in or dropping out at any time. That freedom attracts the young, who, in turn, are much more likely to attract predators. The cases you hear about 14-year-olds rendezvousing with despicable old men begin in chat rooms and rarely from online dating.

All that being said, why take any kind of risk? This chapter shows you how to be a safe and savvy single.

LITTLE WHITE LIES

Ordinary people tell everyday lies. College students tell falsehoods to their moms about half the time, or every other interaction, according to one study. As we age and become more responsible, we tend to be more truthful than we were in our youth. More truthful, but not completely so. Husbands and wives, for example, lie in nearly one out of 10 interactions, according to Bella DePaulo, Ph.D., visiting professor in social psychology at the University of California, Santa Barbara.

For the most part, the reasons for prevaricating with anyone are unthreatening. "People tell everyday lies to try to make themselves look better or feel better, to protect themselves from embarrassment or disapproval or from having their feelings hurt, and to try to gain the esteem and affection of other people," says Dr. DePaulo.

Online daters are not exempt from the run-of-the-mill lying that goes on in real life. Men are more likely to stretch the truth about their height, hair, or physical condition. Women finesse about their age or weight. A bit of wishful thinking goes into these common, idealized fabrications. They may represent the way we were or the way we plan to be.

Flirting a bit with the truth may not seem harmful, but it can be hurtful. At the very least, overediting or embellishing a profile and falsifying information in an e-mail can waste someone's time. More than that, it violates the foundation that makes Internet dating unique.

One of the underpinnings of the Cycle of Rapport (see chapter 8) is a gradual disclosure of the true self. Liars—even those who tell little ones—therefore cheat themselves. As Dr. DePaulo explains, "When people lie about who they are and how they really feel, they cannot elicit understanding or validation of the person they really believe themselves to be."

In other words, they sabotage the very reason for going online in the first place: to find acceptance of the "real me."

Lying also short-circuits promising relationships. It's hard to recover trust, to become trust*worthy* again, once a lie is eventually uncovered. Even a tiny untruth can be of great significance over time. Dr. DePaulo speculates that romantic relationships that ultimately result in marriage are characterized by greater honesty from the outset.

Truth is best, and it's wise to be on the lookout for the clues on the following pages that point to a hard-core problem with truthfulness.

BIG FAT LIARS
How the Truth Sleuths Spot Them

There are telltale signs that someone may not be on the up-and-up. Dr. DePaulo, who has studied deception for more than 20 years, offers these hints:

↗ Extroverts and highly sociable people tend to tell more lies and tell them better than introverts do. Their lies are usually nonthreatening, even flattering. But the gloss factor may become a problem if the person is inauthentic much of the time.

↗ Manipulative people see lying as an acceptable way of getting what they want. They may be smooth and charmingly likable. Look past the charm to see if there are real values there.

↗ People who are very concerned with the impression they make—narcissists, for example—lie to make themselves look better. Be sure his ego is under control.

↗ Downright dirty liars are evasive and indirect. Their correspondence may be brief and lacking in specific details. They may complain a lot and use the past tense. Habitual liars also tend to make negative statements, points out Dr. DePaulo. They will say "I am not a crook" rather than "I am honest."

Keeping a copy of e-mails and reading them carefully is the best way to steer clear of the dishonest. Look for inconsistencies and exaggerations. Ask for clarity when something seems vague or doesn't make sense. If the answers still sound iffy, delete, delete, delete. Or ask some point-blank questions before you agree to continue corresponding. These questions may seem uncomfortably nosy, but if you're the least bit suspicious, it's better to risk discomfort than to waste more time. And it's certainly smart to know the answers before you meet someone you're unsure about.

"Have you told the truth about your appearance?"

"Are you married? Can I call your home?"

"What makes you angry or upset?"

"Have you ever been in trouble with the law?"

"Are you employed now? Can I verify that?"

"Is there something you're afraid to tell me? I'd rather know about it now."

SPOTTING THE MARRIED MAN

Sites are clamping down on the unfaithful. True.com, for example, verifies marital status by screening members through public records. Others, I expect, will adopt that technology. Meanwhile, here are some clues worth investigating.

Missing information. He doesn't have a photo posted because he doesn't want to be recognized. He won't give out his home or work number because he doesn't want a wife or colleagues to know what he's up to. He's elusive about his last name, where he lives, or his background.

Control issues. He made first contact and insists on calling you. He sets up the dates so he doesn't get noticed. Don't ask to meet his friends or family. He'll keep you very far away from them. ▸

If he passes the written exam and you decide he's someone you'd like to meet, there are still some telltale signs to observe in face-to-face encounters. Liars tip their hands with these cues, according to psychologist Richard Wiseman, Ph.D., of Hertfordshire University:

- Abnormal rate of speech, either very slow or unusually fast
- Frequent speech hesitancies, such as hemming and hawing, pausing too long before answering a question, or giving short answers
- Softer speech or a low-pitched voice
- Inconsistent stories or sounding overly rehearsed
- Odd eye contact, such as gazing downward or not engaging the eyes when smiling
- Moves his head a lot when talking; touches his face more than normal
- Visible signs of tension, such as dilated pupils or sweating. Liars experience fear and guilt when lying.

Trick Photography

When I first laid eyes on Walter, I was delighted that this man, whose personality I'd come to adore through his e-mails, was so much cuter than I'd expected. The photo he'd posted didn't do him justice. Unfortunately, being pleasantly surprised at a first meeting isn't always the case. My friend Hildy was astonished that one of her dates had either posted a photo that was 20 years old or literally aged overnight. Doctored photos are also deceptive. Here's how to get an honest take:

Rule No. 1: No photo, no meeting. Sandy Klein, from chapter 7, took a blind chance on now-husband Greg. I wouldn't be so willing to press my luck. No photo may indicate something to hide, like a marriage, outstanding felony warrant, or 80 pounds that need to go.

Rule No. 2: Ask about age. A man does look good in a tux. He may treasure that shot of himself in formal attire for many years, then dust it off and post it online. Ask innocently, "Nice tux; when was the happy occasion?" Or be matter-of-fact: "How recent is this photo?" If you're very skeptical, request that he e-mail you a photo with a time stamp. Many photo phones and digital cameras have this feature. It's also very common practice to ask for multiple photos. Some sites, such

INTERVIEW WITH THE DATE DETECTIVE

California-licensed private investigator Carmen Naimish specializes in cyber cases, working with clients all over the world. Since she began sleuthing risky romances in 1989, Naimish has heard some pretty tall tales. She stopped one wedding as the bride was headed to church to say her vows. The groom, who Naimish discovered had no means of support, was within minutes of taking the bride for richer and making her poorer. Naimish graciously shared her expertise during a telephone interview.

Q. What do you look for during a typical investigation?

A. Investigations are tailored to meet the concerns of the client. In general, I look for confirmation that the person is who he claims to be. Criminal records are important to search and, as it applies, proof of home ownership, previous marriages, and divorces. A divorce, for example, may be filed but not finalized. If you married a man without that finalization, he would be a bigamist and your marriage most likely null and void.

Q. What are some early warning signs that he's been untruthful?

A. There are typical patterns. Anyone who's secretive or elusive about his past probably has something to hide. He may claim to work for the CIA or other high-security agency, like an anti-terrorist task force, to excuse his secretiveness or unavailability. He may say he has no family to detour you from finding out more about him. One man insisted that he was the reincarnation of an uncle who'd died in a plane crash during the war. They can come up with some dramatic, exciting tales. You can also expect trouble if he blames others, usually the ex-wife, for all his problems. He may say all his relationship failures were the woman's fault. He'll also make sure

as Match.com and SeniorFriendFinder.com, offer photo certification for a fee.

Rule No. 3: Look for photo-shop fakery. Hey, I don't mind losing a few time lines from my own photos, but image enhancement can get so out of hand that you don't have a true picture of a person.

---

you don't try to contact the ex-wife. "She died in a plane crash," he'll say. Or, "She's crazy, and I had to put her in a mental institution." I've heard all of these stories.

Q. These guys sound awful. Why would someone fall for them?

A. They are charming and can be very romantic in the beginning. In fact, beware of someone who professes love right away or gives you expensive gifts early in the relationship. If you have an instinct that something's wrong, you're probably right.

Q. What about money rip-offs, like the bride you mentioned?

A. Mature daters should be cautious because they probably have more assets to lose. Making a loan to a man is highly risky. Don't fall for stories about his losing his wallet or that he's waiting for "funds to transfer."

Q. What else does a savvy single need to know?

A. My motto is, "If you date, investigate." Don't be afraid to ask questions, and keep notes on the answers. Find out his full name, including middle name or initial. And date of birth. Even the month and year are helpful. You could mention the upcoming birthday of a friend, then ask what his is. You also need a current address, preferably his previous address as well. I can then determine which county records should be checked. With this kind of information you can do some detecting yourself at the courthouse.

Q. What if someone wanted to hire you?

A. Call my toll-free number, (888)-84-CHECK. Fees typically begin around $375. My Web site is DateSmart.com.

Switching heads and bodies, for example, is too much digital dilly-dallying.

Professor of computer science Hany Farid, Ph.D., of Dartmouth College, is a leading expert on photo forgery. He says it's difficult to pin-point tampering in small, Web-size photos, but there are a few things to observe:

* If someone looks "plastic" or artificially smooth, he's probably had some techno wrinkle removal.
* Check the chin. "It's hard to fix a double chin," says Dr. Farid. "If it looks odd, he probably attempted a kind of photo liposuction, and it didn't work."
* Ghosting, blurring, or a halo effect (ring around the photo) also points to manipulation.
* If you're a keen observer, you may notice inconsistent lighting and shadows.

Telephone Tips

That first phone call is a big step in e-dating. You're moving the relationship to a new medium and new level. You may be eager to hear his voice, but exercise caution before the calls begin.

* Don't feel pressured into phone contact. I'd suggest waiting at least several weeks. If someone is unusually persistent about talking, it could be a red flag. Is he looking for a quick affair? Is he overly controlling?
* Do ask for his telephone number and make the first call yourself. It will help you verify information and possibly spot a marital cheater. You may want to make the initial call from a public phone.
* Don't give out your home, business, or fax numbers until you really know him. Use a cell phone with caller ID for his incoming calls. Activate the blocking feature on caller ID (usually *67) before dialing out.

Address Advice

There are many online options for sending someone you fancy a greeting card or photo. But there may be instances when you or he wants to use the mail—to send a magazine article about something you discussed, for example. It's easy and inexpensive to get a post office box to handle any offline correspondence. That way you'll have peace of mind about protecting your home and business addresses. (Also see "Pre-Meeting Precautions" on page 147.)

ONLINE DEFENSE:
How to Avoid Harassers and Stalkers

The Internet watchdog organization Working to Halt Online Abuse (WHOA) recorded 198 cases of online harassment and stalking in 2003. Fewer than 200 reported cases among a universe of 37 million online romantics points to how rare (or unreported) this kind of abuse can be. What's more, cyber-victims tend to be young (63 percent in the WHOA sample were between the ages of 18 and 30) and often know their online harasser or stalker (for example, the ex-boyfriend who mailed nude photos of a woman to her boss). Still, as I noted at the beginning of the chapter, why take any chances?

Online dating services, which use an anonymizer to hide your real e-mail address, are your first line of defense. It's easier to stop or switch an account with a service than to change your regular e-mail. Dating services also offer online aid and a blocking feature called decline contact. Be sure to report any kind of annoying correspondence—sites want to get rid of these guys.

Your own good judgment is also important. Don't get involved with sketchy types to begin with: men who are negative, complaining, controlling, jealous, suspicious, hostile to women, too sexy, or too in a hurry to meet. Eliminate them early. Do not even reply to their contact (see chapter 7). "When you respond to a harasser in any way," cautions WHOA, "you're letting him know he has succeeded. He wants a reaction."

Also know the profile of *offline* stalkers. Research shows that they tend to be substance abusers, are often unemployed, and have difficulty forming relationships. Most violent stalkers have had a previous, usually intimate, relationship with their victims. They tend to be husbands, ex-husbands, or boyfriends.

Harassment and stalking, whether online or off, is illegal in most

THE RAPE REPORT

There's not a bright side when it comes to news about rape and assault. These are the crimes women dread and fear. It's not much comfort to know that as we age we become safer, while our daughters may be at their most vulnerable, but it is important to know the facts. These statistics reflect all rape/assault cases, as there is no available record on Internet dating site–related crimes.

⬈ About 44 percent of rape victims are under age 18, and 80 percent are under age 30. The median age for rape/sexual assault is 23.

⬈ Ages 12 to 34 are the highest-risk years. Girls 16 to 19 are four times more likely than the general population to be victims of rape, attempted rape, or sexual assault.

⬈ The average age of rapists at arrest is 31.

⬈ Two-thirds of sexual assaults are committed by someone known to the victim—friends, acquaintances, intimates, even family members.

⬈ Acquaintance rapists are bullying and controlling. This kind of man may make belittling and insulting comments, sit too close, or touch a woman when she tells him not to. He may insist on picking the restaurant, get angry if the woman offers to pay, berate her if she refuses to get drunk or go with him to his apartment or hers.

⬈ More than half of all rape/assault incidents take place within the victim's home or within one mile of the home. ⬉

instances. Contact your local law-enforcement agency if you've been harassed or stalked, as many localities now have special units to handle such complaints.

Don't Advertise for Trouble

Studies show that our mothers were right. A marriage-minded man wants a woman who is respectable, according to John Molloy's research; and one who is warm, not hot, according to Dr. Woll.

Review your profile and questionnaire to be sure you've avoided come-ons and steamy handles, such as SEXYMAMA or 69-4U. Overly romantic writing is an indicator of vulnerability, so steer clear of it as well—you don't want to come across as an easy target. Provocative or sentimental photos may also entice the wrong kind of person. For success and safety, present yourself in word and image as a vital winner—not a sexy sap (refer back to chapter 4).

Where you advertise is also important. Reputable online dating services offer the most protection (see chapter 6). You take a much bigger risk on sites that clearly cater to wild sex interests.

PRE-MEETING PRECAUTIONS

If you took the route of gradual disclosure, you've had many weeks to get to know this man through his e-mails and your phone calls. You've explored each other's values, education, family background, interests, and life goals. He passed your lie-detecting tests, and you're pretty sure you have an honest psychological and physical picture of him. I think you're ready to meet face-to-face, with just a few last-minute safety checks.

Stay away from home. You don't want to disclose your address yet. Pick a public spot to meet and be seen. A coffee shop or bookstore is a good idea. Avoid parks or bike trails for now.

Use your own transportation. You need your wheels so you can leave the date when you're ready.

Avoid alcohol. Almost half of assaults occur while the perpetrator is under the influence of alcohol, according to RAINN, the National Sexual Assault Hotline. Alcohol also clouds *your* judgment and responses. If you do decide to imbibe, never leave your cocktail unattended. Ask for a fresh drink when you return from the bathroom, for example, to avoid having it spiked with a knockout drug.

Inform a friend. She should know where and when you're meeting him. Give her a copy of his profile with photo and user name, his real full name, and phone number. Have her call you on your cell phone at an appointed time. If you want an easy escape, you can then tell your date something like, "I'm sorry to cut this short, but I'm needed at home."

Have Date, Will Travel

Setting up a long-distance rendezvous requires complete safety awareness. Be sure to review and internalize all the expert safety advice in this chapter. Ask questions. Clarify. Ask again.

If you're visiting him, make the travel arrangements yourself, including your hotel reservation. (You weren't thinking of staying with him, were you?) Discuss in advance what will happen if the chemistry isn't right for either of you. My friend Julie realized on a Friday night that she really didn't like a guy. She felt an obligation to stick out the weekend, but what torture. It would have been easier on both of them to agree on an amicable no-fault parting pact ahead of time. Then she might have at least enjoyed sightseeing on her own.

If he's visiting you, dodge your favorite watering holes. If perchance he's not the one, you don't want to spoil your best spots with a bad memory or let him know where you hang out.

♦

I don't want this chapter to scare you, and I hope it hasn't. I feel a responsibility, however, to make sure you're well informed about even the remotest risks, and they *are* remote. I believe that an Internet date can be the safest date you ever make. With good screening and good judgment, you can be more in control than you would from a random meeting or blind date. Be savvy, be safe, and have fun!

RESOURCES

Helpful links to find out more information:

↗ **CyberAngels.org:** A program of the Guardian Angels; advice on cyberstalking and other Internet crimes

↗ **haltabuse.org:** A Web site for Working to Halt Online Abuse (WHOA); tracks cyber-crimes and offers resources and how-tos

↗ **ojp.usdoj.gov:** U.S. Department of Justice, Office of Justice Programs, Bureau of Justice Statistics

↗ **RAINN.org:** National Sexual Assault Hotline, (800) 656-HOPE; statistics, information, counseling centers

↗ **Saferdating.com:** Do's and don'ts of Internet dating

↗ **SelfhelpMagazine.com:** Cyber-safety tips

↗ **WiredSafety.org:** The world's largest Internet safety, help, and education organization

↗ **WhoIsHe.Com:** Cheap background investigations using public records (similar service: KnowX.com). Prices start at $1 but can climb. ↖

READY
TO MEET

You have two competitive advantages as a midlife online dater: maturity and your online sneak preview.

At first, maturity may not seem like much of a benefit. You might feel darn silly courting—online dating, even—at your age. I know in the beginning I felt a little odd going out on dates just like my daughter. My single friends who are grandparents say they felt an initial reluctance, too. Shouldn't they be on call for babysitting? On the other hand, my widowed mother, a great-grandmother, has an envious dating life and not an ounce of doubt. She'd tell you the silly thing would be to sit home when you could be at the symphony with a charming man.

Here's one more reason not to fret about what a woman your age should or should not be doing: there's never been such a block of mature singles in modern American history. As I said in the introduction, there's a Boomer Date Quake. Just as in the early years, when Boomers all watched *Howdy Doody*, we change the culture by sheer force of our numbers. ThirdAge Personals, a site for Boomers, has over 20 million page views each month. That kind of volume suggests this is now a mainstream activity.

When you join the ranks of the other courting Boomers, you'll discover that dating is different this time around. Your skills may be a bit rusty—we can fix that here—but think of all the life experience maturity has given you. Aren't you more discerning now and a better judge of character? Wiser and more warmhearted? Haven't your years of working and dealing with all kinds of people taught you to be both tactful *and* assertive? See, you're better equipped for dating, in the ways that matter, than you possibly could have been in your teens.

Remember your other advantage. As an online dater, you are able to prequalify your candidates. You know your date is in the market for a relationship. It's as if a sales manager handed you a list of prospects: "Here are the people who say they're definitely interested in buying. I've talked with them a dozen times about it. They've even filled out the paperwork."

Furthermore, as you e-mailed, you initiated the Cycle of Rapport. He has revealed himself, more than he ever would in the bright lights of reality, and because he has shown you some of the inner self, he is predisposed to liking you.

So not only is he in the market for a relationship, he's in the market

FOUR INSTANT STRESS RELIEVERS

You may be nervous at first, but dating does get easier on you. In the meantime, don't tell yourself you're nervous. Try what psychologists call "adaptive relabeling." Say to yourself instead: "I'm excited about meeting someone new. It's a challenge, but it will get better with practice." Also try these easy tips:

↗ **Smile.** The brain doesn't register stress when you smile, and it's a powerful flirting tool.

↗ **Yawn (though not in front of him).** It's a quick way to gather oxygen and dump anxiety.

↗ **Tongue trick.** Speech coaches suggest circling your tongue around your inner lips a few times to relieve dry mouth.

↗ **Chew gum.** Again, not in front of him. But a stick ahead of time helps you to relax, according to research. Ask any ballplayer or cow how calming it is to chew. ↖

for a relationship with you or someone just like you. You're the model he wants. Your meeting is the test drive. And, of course, you're also assessing him.

This chapter will help you through the test drive. You'll feel more confident and comfortable with every aspect of dating.

DRESS AND GROOMING:
Prepare for the Dating Scene

There are many, many things more important than appearance. Don't make it an excuse for sitting home. On the other hand, you may want to perk up a bit. Perhaps you're out of practice dressing up or looking your best for someone else. These tips will give you a fresh start and self-assured attitude.

Clothing Confidence

Maybe you're one of those lucky women who have a natural-born sense of style. My sister Jennifer is like that. Everything she wears, even down to her gym socks, looks fashionable and perfect on her.

When I started courting, I knew I had to work on my very imperfect style and invest in a dating wardrobe. I needed some new looks for fun and romance.

The first step in my fashion makeover: get a better attitude. I really hate to bother with clothes. I dislike shopping, selecting an outfit for an occasion—the whole bit. But I know appearance is important, especially when you're trying to be as attractive as possible. Despite my laziness and loathing, I became a dutiful shopper. I soon found brands, like Ellen Tracy and Eileen Fisher, that always seem to offer smart and sensual looks for a woman my age—and their clothes are available at outlets. I also have great luck with the Isaac Mizrahi line at Target. Narrowing down the shopping game to a couple of brands and a couple of stores made it easier for me.

Step two in my dress-better quest: out with the old. Everything in my closet fell into two categories: work and wear-around-the-house. The work stuff stayed, but all my bulky sweatshirts, stodgy shoes, and pants that made me look frumpy had to go. Too many of my things stereotyped me as a matronly mom. I was thankful that I didn't buy the expensive Christmas reindeer sweater I once considered, but plenty of other atrocities were hanging around. I had to get rid of this dowdy stuff because I knew it would find a way to creep back onto my body. The cozy recidivist in me would be talked into wearing the baggy khakis with the bleach spots on the knees. The comfort clothes would destroy my budding coolness if I were not careful. Needless to say, my entire underwear drawer was dumped. And I swear to you, I really don't miss the maternity panties that were still in there.

Step three: find attractive activewear. Most mature men rate physical fitness more highly than sexiness. I'm with them, and I believe that a great sports outfit *is* sexy. It shows spirit, vitality, and a joy in the physical self. Many of my dates involved hiking, skiing, golfing, swimming, or working out. Instead of putting on any old ratty thing just because there might be some sweat involved, I took care to select flattering outfits. I had Katharine Hepburn's image in mind. I tried to go for that look: well-bred tomboy chic. It worked for me.

Thus ends my personal fashion wisdom. The experts say don't be too dressy or too casual, and avoid showing skin. Pink-peach is supposed to be the most flattering color to wear. Medium blue is the most friendly and sincere. Red is powerful but can be intimidating. I'm sure any of your favorite colors—except perhaps yellow-green, which can make you look sallow—will be just fine.

What to wear should not be a roadblock you set up for yourself. In fact, according to my well-dressed friend Jan Pike, it's important to be who you are. "If you dress in a way that's not you," she points out, "you'll start a relationship off on false footing, and you might be so uncomfortable that you won't act like yourself, either."

Maybe you're simply lackadaisical, like me, and just need to energize your wardrobe. It will give you confidence. Update to be ready to date up a storm.

What's Beautiful after 35?

I might not have inherited a sense of fashion, but I did get my mother's skin. We both prize a good complexion and take great care of ours. When I play golf, for example, I don't wear sunscreen. I wear *blackout* cream that not a ray of sunshine can penetrate. My mother taught me early on about sun damage. Mother and I are also huge advocates of Avon skin care. Recently she ran out of their Retroactive Repair Cream, and I had some shipped to her next-day air. We have our priorities, and moisturizing is one of them.

There are so many products and processes that help skin look fresh and healthy. I advise visiting a dermatologist as faithfully as you would your gynecologist: to check for skin cancer, most importantly, but also to have a little talk about younger-looking skin. Your next stop should be the beauty counters at your department store. I make a beeline for MAC or Bobbi Brown, but any brand that's offering a makeover is worth a visit. The tips can be inspiring and even refreshing or revitalizing.

Hair is also the great updater. I was stuck in a blunt-cut rut for a good 25 years. My short, layered hair seems friskier to me, but some of my friends look smashing in long styles à la Jackie Kennedy. I tried going gray when I turned 50. I may try it again 30 years from now. In the meantime I'm sticking with highlights.

Only 10 percent of Boomers say they want to look *as young as possible*, according to a Yankelovich Monitor survey. However, 57 percent want to look *young for their age*. Here are hair and makeup switches from *Allure* and other magazines that can help you meet that goal, and maybe even drop a decade:

Younger	Older
Subtle eye shadow shades (beige or toffee)	Dark, smoky, or bright blue shadow
Charcoal, navy, or chocolate eyeliner	Black eyeliner
Eyeliner on upper lashes only	Heavy "raccoon eyes"
Tinted lip gloss	Bright red lips
Cream blush/light touch	Powder blush/deep contours
Well-manicured nails	Claws for nails
Sheer, pale pink nail color	Frosted, dark brown, or red nails
Straight, touchable hair	Stiff hairdo (aka "helmet head")
Gentle curls	"Poodle perm"
Swingy haircut with bangs	One-length bob
Hair highlights	Gray hair
Blend of colors	Single-process color ("bottle blonde")

Clean and Smiling

Good grooming and good hygiene demonstrate your self-esteem. Whatever you choose to wear, make sure it's fresh and neat. Keep nails and hair trimmed, roots and dandruff treatments up-to-date. An antiperspirant, especially if you feel anxious, is a must.

Dental care is a key concern after 35. Teeth tend to shift and need watching to stay aligned. I got braces at 48 to correct my Bucky Beaver overbite. My mother followed my example and was fitted at 72. I really enjoy my straight teeth; they're one of the youngest things about me. And now there are orthodontic breakthroughs like Invisalign that are almost impossible to detect. Whitening products, applied at home or at the dentist's office, subtract years. Also be sure the dentist checks you for bad-breath factors such as periodontal disease or tongue bacteria. A sinus infection or acid reflux may contribute to bad breath, too.

You may think perfume is a turn-on, but it has an equal chance of turning men off. In fact, many people put a heavy scent in the same category as cigarette smoke. Go lightly, if you wear it at all.

We Have to Talk about Body *a Little Bit*

The research shows, and the men I interviewed verify, that physical appearance isn't the most important factor in a man's choice. Age keeps us all humble, and "a little padding," as one questionnaire describes it, is not necessarily a deficit. Many men, in fact, are too focused on their own love handles to worry about yours.

The requirement that does come across loud and strong, however, is healthiness. For example, when I scanned profiles with a friend in Alabama, every third man mentioned fitness. Not one insisted on a drop-dead figure. Men simply wanted someone who would (1) take care of herself and (2) try to look her best.

You don't have to be in perfect shape to win approval. But it will help as you meet men to have at least a foot in the door of a fitness program. As I suggested to my friend, "If you joined a gym and started working out, your pool of candidates would increase by a third or more." Stamina and self-esteem would also rise. Plus, fitness makes for good conversation, and gym dates can be fun.

The best fitness program is the one you'll do. Fifteen years ago I went to a spa and decided I loved feeling exercised, rejuvenated, and pampered in a healthful way. I realized I could live spalike on my own (massages and facials being the exception). It was easy to find inexpensive water aerobics and body sculpting/stretch classes similar to the ones I'd enjoyed at the $350-a-day resort. When I think of exercise as a treat, not a chore, I'm eager to do it.

As for diet, I like the way my body feels and works and looks when I indulge in spalike foods. By that I mean cutting back on fats and adding more whole grains and beautiful, colorful fruits and vegetables to my plate. With a glass of fresh-squeezed orange juice and my standard morning fare (a bowl of very-high-fiber Bran Buds mixed with warm blueberries, cranberries, cherries, and a big dollop of low-fat yogurt), I feel transported back to spa bliss. These foods happen to help lower cholesterol and fight osteoporosis and cancer, too. Spa-ful eating also includes seeds and nuts; dark green and yellow veggies like spinach and yellow peppers; and low-cal, low-fat dressings. Of the latter, I found a brand, Up Country Organics Balsamic Vinaigrette, which has me eating salads like crazy. It tastes so much better than other fat-free choices, and two tablespoons have only five calories. A regular dressing has close to 200 calories, so if you eat a salad every day, a dressing switch could save 71,175 calories, or 20 pounds a year. Nutritionists say that losing just 10 percent of body mass protects against diabetes and heart disease. Those 20 pounds could be more than your 10 percent.

You may also recall that spas push water and curtail caffeine, alcohol, and nicotine. The water strategy helps rid the body of these toxins, the same culprits often blamed for change-of-life complaints plus most other bad things. Along with more water every day, I'd also take two flaxseed-oil gelcaps, my favorite toxin-reducing, weight-loss secret weapon. How does the flaxseed work? As my trim friend Margaret Kenrick advises, "It's all a process of elimination."

Diet and exercise also affect sexuality. As you tone up, you look better and feel more self-assured and desirable. Exercise also relieves symptoms associated with perimenopause and menopause. It improves circulation (to ease hot flashes), promotes better sleep, and may naturally increase your supply of the important hormone estrogen.

The majority of Boomers, according to a Yankelovich Monitor survey, say they are working to improve—or would like to be working on improving—the shape of their bodies (73 percent), their diet (71 percent), and their self-image (60 percent). This could be the day you begin that project. As an incentive, visit Livingto100.com, which has a quiz to help you determine your longevity. The answers include health, diet, and fitness tips to improve your score.

FIRST DATE:
Where and When

Before you agree to get together, you should think about two categories of meetings. The first is a mini-date, an encounter with a quick exit strategy. This category works for practice dates, or Courtship Contenders that you're considering but need to meet face-to-face before continuing the communication. Schedule mini-dates for week-days. Suggest lunch, or coffee after work. That way, if he's off your list,

ISN'T IT ROMANTIC?

Successful online daters are practical optimists—hopeful realists that often know right away when a match is a good one.

Betsy, in her late 40s, was an experienced dater who set up her first date with Nick so that it would last only an hour. "The hour rushed by, and I couldn't stop thinking about him after we parted," she says. "I called him and asked if we could get together later that evening, and he said yes. It felt like we had always known each other. In the first couple of weeks, I knew I was going to be with him for the rest of my life, and he felt the same way. My friends had a good feeling about us, too. They predicted Nick and I were going to be married. I was divorced for twenty years, but I married Nick less than six months after meeting him. What a wonderful surprise at my age. He is the love of my life—unquestionably—and I am his."

"I received hundreds of profiles and e-mails," writes Linda, "but I only responded to one—Jeff's. It spoke volumes to me. I felt we could share our real selves with each other, and we were perfectly matched. We e-mailed and phoned for over a month before seeing each other face-to-face. When I got out of the car, our eyes met, we came together, and without saying a word he cupped my face in his hands and kissed me softly on the lips before our first word of hello. We haven't been apart one day since, and were married eighteen months after that first kiss."

After a month of e-mailing, 53-year-old Nina felt her online partner,

you're both out only a few bucks and an hour or so of your time. If he is a hit, you can set up date two.

For someone with soul-mate potential, try an add-on date, one that can expand if you really click. A New Jersey couple, Doug and Nancy, met for a movie and quick bite. The 50-year-olds got along so well, however, that the quick bite evolved into a long, leisurely dinner, then dessert and coffee. They called it a night only when the proprietor started vacuuming the floor around them.

Couples also arrange first dates around common interests. Pam and

now her husband, was someone she'd known forever. "The first time we met, we were so honest with each other, and there was a real sense of familiarity, no desperation at all. I met my past relationships the old-fashioned way, and they certainly were a bust. Now I can say I've found my best friend of all time."

After his first date with Donna, Eric Frank told his best friend, "I think I've found someone." Ten months later he confirmed his initial instinct, proposing to her on February 1 (2/1), a date that in his mind symbolized two into one. During a romantic dinner, he presented her a series of candy hearts that said "Kiss me," "I love you," and, finally, "Marry me." Later, when the couple went outside, they were surprised to see that an ice storm had passed by. "The moon was so bright," says Eric, "and it looked as if the silvery trees were cued up just for us."

Cyber-lovers are sentimental about the first meeting and everything else that's part of the online romance. Walter's e-mail to me after our first date graced the back of our wedding program. Stephanie Fischer read one of husband Jim's e-mails during their ceremony. Sandy Klein and Greg Thoma staged a play about their computer match-up for wedding guests. Sarah Hutter and Eric Frank collected all the e-mail messages from their courtship days and created books as valentine gifts for their mates. This newfangled way of dating brings out some old-fashioned emotions.

Michael Pierre (from chapter 7) first saw each other at a dirt-track racing event. Sharing an activity is certainly a way to feel more at ease. Concerts and loud bars don't offer an opportunity to talk—why go there?

DRINKING AND DINING
(And Paying the Bill)

A bar and restaurant is a classic courting site. Quiet, cozy ones are made for conversation and gazing eye-to-eye. They work especially well for add-on dates. There are a couple of caveats, however.

Go easy on the alcohol. As noted in the last chapter, most assailants say that they were under the influence of alcohol or drugs at the time of their crime. So watch his drinking. As for yours, drink as little as possible. You may think it helps you relax, but what happens is that it muddles your judgment and kicks in a very unattractive mush-mouth way of speaking. Stick to one wine spritzer or a weak water-and-Scotch. This is not the time to test your capacity for high-octane apple martinis or cosmos. Finally, don't be teased or coerced into exceeding your limit. A date that would do that doesn't have your best interests in mind.

Give food some thought. Dishes with lots of garlic and onion may linger on your breath. Corn and seeds may linger between your teeth. Ribs and lobster can be messy and hard to handle. On the other hand, at our age we've earned the right to dig in and enjoy a spicy or messy meal. If your date orders garlicky bread sticks or scampi, that's your cue to relax and enjoy anything on the menu; you can scarf down breath mints later. The best date I ever had was the second one with my husband. We were up to our elbows in blue crabs and garlicky black-bean sauce. Our table was a wreck, piled high with crab shells, thick with juice. At one point Walter pointed to his teeth, cuing me that I had black beans embedded in mine. We'd certainly abandoned the Emily Post conduct practiced on our first date, and, boy, did we have fun.

Decide in advance who pays. When I dated in my 20s, I made it a rule to split the bill. Paying my share helped me decide if I truly liked a guy: Was it worth forking over my meager dollars to be with him? It also meant I had no obligation to him; that is, no implied quid pro quo for sexual favors. In my dating life, round two, I amended the rule. I still offered to pay or at least pick up the tip, or pay the next time. But I didn't get into battles for the bill. Men my age had had enough time to mellow into gentlemen. To them, paying was a sign of politeness, nothing more, and protesting too much actually hurt their feelings, as if I were rejecting a gift—and them. You're mature enough to make your own rules. If you decide the man always pays, be gracious and sensitive to his budget, but that's all you owe him, except a thank-you note or e-mail.

FLIRTING, PART I:
Your Body Language

Before you say anything, your body says everything. A man can read your interest or disinterest from the way you stand, smile, look (or don't look) him in the eye. Extroverts are usually skilled at exhibiting flirtatious body language, which is why they're more popular people, but anyone can get better at some aspects of it. Even mud turtles, according to scientists, know how to flirt. You can do this!

Begin with your stance. Standing straight and tall looks confident and appealing, and you probably need to stand this way anyway to keep your stomach in. Check out your posture in the mirror. Also note your feet. They should be about six inches apart, with your toes pointing slightly inward. Now lean forward a bit. These are the universal signals that you're approachable.

I make a couple of body language mistakes when I'm standing, and I know they're off-putting. One is that I fold my arms across the chest, which is interpreted as "back off." What I'm really trying to say is, "Why don't they adjust the air conditioning in here? I'm freezing." An obvious solution is to wear a jacket or light sweater. I also put my hands on my hips, the way mothers do when they want a child to "come in the house this minute!" It's certainly less hostile looking when I remember to keep my arms unfolded and hands loosely by my side.

Use your eyes. I suppose the coy ploy of batting the eyelashes can be learned. I grew up in Mobile, Alabama, and if someone's ever going to learn that particular skill, I think Mobile would be the place to do it. Somehow I never got the hang of it, though my three-year-old great-niece Gracie already has it mastered. I don't wink well, either, and I find it impossible to arch my brow in a seductive way, especially if the Botox is working.

For those of us who can't bat, wink, or arch, there's always "gluing the eyes" on the intended. Anthropologist Helen Fisher, Ph.D., says in *Anatomy of Love* that the female possum knows this trick: She turns "toward her suitor, cocking her snouty jaw, and [looks] straight into his eyes." I may be a failed Southern belle in some ways, but here's an area where I know I can at least beat out a possum.

To glue your eyes on a man, simply maintain eye contact while he speaks, and then—this is how to one-up the possum—hold that contact even after he finishes speaking and slowly break away. You'll find this kind of ultra eye contact is an easy and effective courting art.

Get ready to smile. A great smile shows friendliness and interest. It's one of the best ways to make the all-important positive first impression. There is a little secret to smiling, however. One day, when I was editing old television tapes for my Web site, I noticed that if I began a segment with a huge smile I sometimes seemed silly. Like *Mad* magazine's Alfred E. Newman, I looked as if I needed a sign over my head saying, "Why is this woman smiling?" I realized a pre-smile followed by a gradual beam is much more attractive. The pre-smile is a pleasant thought that lights up your face and shows in your eyes. For example, at that initial contact think to yourself, "I'm about to meet a man who's interested in me, and we're going to have a fabulous time." Get your pre-smile working, move toward him, shake hands, glue eyes (see possum pointers)—and then launch your beamer, a big, toothy (uppers and lowers showing) grin. Use the pre-smile/smile throughout your conversation to demonstrate you're in sync.

Touch lightly. Be careful of physical contact during a first encounter. You may be meeting a pawing sort of person, and the slightest encouraging pat on your part may send him into touchy-feely high gear. If he's not a mauling type—and you'll know right away—it's safe to send him some tactile valentines: a quick touch on his hand or shoulder, for example; or your leg may find a way to rub up against his for a split second. The goodbye touch is up to you. A kiss on the cheek or friendly embrace indicates you'd like a second date. Anything less is probably a relationship ender; before trying anything more, read chapter 12.

His Body Language

Your body isn't the only one that's busy communicating. His eyes will give you the once-over or twice-over if he's interested. His eyebrows may raise while you're talking, another positive indicator. If he leads you to the table by placing his hand on the small of your back and moves closer to you as you talk, you definitely have his attention. Catch him sucking in his stomach, and I think you've got him. Eager courtiers also fiddle with their clothes and hair, according to Tracey Cox in her book *Superflirt*. He may smooth his tie and hair. A super sign of acceptance, according to Cox, is if he pulls up his socks. That telegraphs that he wants to look good for you, right down to his toes.

FLIRTING, PART II:
Conversation

The first thing you may be wondering is, "What shall we talk about?" You can start with a compliment: "You look so much more handsome in real life." Or, "I was so interested in meeting you, because your profile . . . " If you're reluctant to begin that way, the weather is actually not a bad opener. But flattery and meteorology will only get you so far. You need to have some topics ready for discussion.

You may want to try the trick celebrities use before interviews. They prepare sound bites—interesting conversational tidbits—so they won't be flustered and searching for words on camera. What impressed you in his e-mails? There should be lots of good material to probe in there. Be ready to talk about your favorite movies and music (see chapter 5), a current event, sports (see chapter 1), and your work and interests. Recall some of your classic moments growing up and something funny that happened to you recently—humor is high on everyone's list of favorite traits.

Think of the first meeting as an interview for a friendship. What do you have in common? Can you have fun together? In the following chapters, you'll discover why the friendship factor is more important than trying to figure out whether this is the *man of your dreams*. The true dream man, according to research, is your best friend.

To keep things congenial on that first date, don't talk about politics or religion. You probably have a good sense of how he stands on those subjects from your discussions online. If you met on a religion-oriented site, I'm sure you disclosed your level of observance. But religion and politics are personal powder kegs. It's well known that people within the same congregation or political party often disagree. Why set off a potential explosive? Keep it cool. When you know this person better, then, if you need to, you can have an informed debate.

Three other taboo topics: family dramas, complaints about other men, and money. This first meeting is a chance to check each other out in an amiable way face-to-face. As I mentioned, your previous correspondence has granted you a favored status position. If you want to pass this closer inspection, however, don't lose your advantage. Stay positive, even when it's tempting to share with an empathetic adult the intriguing details of your teenager's court appearance. The best thing to say about an old relationship: "We're friends now." As for money, don't boast about your financial success with talk about expensive vacations or your second home. (Avoid those other symbols of wealth, fine jewelry and furs, too.) The same applies if your balance sheet is more in the red than the black these days. It's the rare man who wants to take on someone else's financial burden.

Just as important as what you say or don't say is how you listen. Here's your chance to discover more about this person, with all the body language and nuance you missed in e-mail. Don't listen with half an ear, and don't interrupt. To let him know he has your attention, repeat some of what he has said back to him. Follow up with how, why, or what questions, rather than ones that can be answered with a yes or no. A "no" can start a negative spiral. For example:

"Oh, you like the Cubs. Did you watch the game last night?"

If he says no, your conversation thread is over. Better:

"I hear what you're saying about the Cubs. How did they become your favorite team?"

Master listeners also know how to figure out his favorite way of being understood. He'll give you the clues soon after you meet.

An auditory type loves to talk. He's articulate and expressive. To let him know you're interested in what he's telling you, use phrases such as "I hear what you're saying" or "Listen to this."

The visual guy will notice details about the restaurant and what you're wearing. He may talk quickly. Get his attention by complimenting the tie he's wearing. "I really like that pattern and color." Say "I see what you mean," "Picture this," or "I've never looked at it that way."

The kinesthetic person likely spends time at the gym. You may catch him flexing his muscles or cracking his knuckles. He processes information through touch and feel, so touch his hand lightly to get an important point across. He also responds to emotional words: "That feels right to me" or "I share your feelings."

As your conversation continues, you may notice that you're starting to mirror each other's actions. When you tilt your head, he tilts his. When you lean in closer, he does, too. If you talk a bit more softly, which is very seductive, he listens more intently.

The rapport that began online is surviving the rigors of a reality check.

GOOD NIGHTS OR GOODBYES

Your first date is going well. You'd like a second for sure. You caught him pulling up his socks, so you know there's interest on his part. How do you end the evening with a promise of more? Chapter 4 discussed sales techniques, and one of them comes into play now: *Ask for the business*. Get the order for the next date. Simply say, "Being with you was fun. I hope we get together again."

Here is why I think those little words are important. The mature man is vulnerable. Unless he's one of the 2.3 million never-married men ages 45 to 64, he's a widower or divorced. Bachelorhood was not the early plan for his life. He has experienced loss, disillusion, and hurt, and what he fears most is rejection. I know you can identify with those feelings. Make courtship easier on him. Take some of the guesswork out of it.

If you're definitely not interested in the guy and never will be (see the next chapter, "Chemistry and Sex"), don't pretend that there's more in store. A handshake and goodbye are rather clear "no progress" signals. If he presses his luck and asks you out right then, there are a few kinds of ego-preserving exit lines:

Not enough in common: "I was so curious to meet you, and your stories about Nepal were fascinating. But I think we're at opposite extremes when it comes to what we like to do."

Still searching: "Thanks. I'm very flattered. I've just started online dating, though, and I'm still kind of flighty. It would be in both of our interests if I didn't take up your time."

Busy: "I have a heavy travel schedule ahead of me for the next few weeks. Let me consider it and get back to you."

If you get flustered, it's okay to send a follow-up escape e-mail the next day, when you've had a chance to think of something kind, nonjudgmental, and definitive to say. Don't let your natural niceness prolong the inevitable, however. That may not turn out to be a nice gesture after all.

Cathy, in Dallas, for example, was out with a rapid-hands man and didn't know how to curb his enthusiasm. To get out of the awful evening, she suggested a date for a bike ride later in the week. When he showed up all ready to roll, he confessed that he'd spent two nights on the Internet researching the Midwestern area where she grew up. "Oh my," she thought, "this is getting worse. Time to bail." Did he appreciate her earlier attempt to spare his feelings? No good deed goes unpunished, as they say. He was irate that she'd led him on and wasted his time.

REFLECTION ON REJECTION

It's true—you won't experience rejection if you stay home safely curled up on the sofa to watch a good movie. Vulnerability, unfortunately, is the price of admission to real-life love stories.

It's easy to say don't take rejection personally. Of course you will, to some extent. It's natural to feel a bit disappointed or lacking when someone you liked well enough to meet doesn't call or your e-mails just aren't answered. Take it as a lesson in personal growth, however, not as an indictment of your personality or powers of attraction. Try to move your thoughts from pain to motivation, from the negative to the positive: What can I learn from this? Is there something I want to do better? What's going on with my judgment? And, remember, Internet dating creates so many choices that it invites nit-picking. The guy who used to settle for any warm body within a 20-mile radius of his small town in Iowa is now checking out babes in Australia. It cuts both ways. Get back online and pick another guy.

SECOND DATE:
The Date of Discovery

You were pretty sure of his interest, and you made it easy for him to ask you out. If he doesn't call in a day or two, or let's say a week or so if he's busy, you may have read the evening wrong or he may have an unidentified agenda. It's doubtful he'll call. If he does surprise you, ringing up weeks or months later, expect more and more games and surprises from Mysterious-Motive Man. Count it as a practice date and move on. (See "Reflection on Rejection" on page 167.)

But let's say everything about the first date went right. The conversation flowed, and he was practically yanking at his socks. You knew he would call, and he did, right away.

Welcome to the second date.

The first date was all about fun. The second date is a discovery mission. Is the friendliness and maybe the chemistry you experienced on date one the real thing or superficial? Without the excitement and anxiety of that first meeting, you can relax and evaluate more clearly.

A dinner date gives you plenty of time to talk more extensively, especially if you first met for lunch or coffee. The spot he selects will tell if he's thoughtful and interested. Is it a restaurant with food you've said you like? Is it romantic? Convenient for you? The date should be important enough for him to plan it well and get there on time.

There are other nonverbal signs, things that wouldn't come across online. Is he self-confident around others? How does he deal with the waiter, for example? (Note: Self-confidence isn't rudeness.) Do the foods he orders and clothes he wears reflect someone who takes care of himself and has high self-esteem? Are your manners compatible (even if you're cracking crabs)?

Try not to be overly judgmental. You can buy him new ties on his birthday, for Pete's sake. But do look for cues to a fit that is psychologically and socially right for you, and focus on how you feel with him. Is he enthusiastic? Attentive? Are you still having fun? Could he be a best friend?

In conversation, take a few risks at self-disclosure (more on this coming up). If you've corresponded and disclosed gradually online, it will be new to see how he shares face-to-face, without the privacy, protection, and anonymity of the Internet. Is he as willing to reveal himself as he was when you couldn't hear and see each other?

Sarah and Andrew Get It Right

After a few weeks of e-mailing on Match.com, Sarah Hutter met Andrew Hess for a quick drink at Ocean, a Caribbean-inspired seafood restaurant on Manhattan's Upper West Side. Although their first face-to-face introduction lasted only an hour, it was enough time to feel an instant attraction and share a few laughs before Andrew had to jump on the subway and head back to Brooklyn.

Their second date, for a movie and then dinner at an Indian restaurant, gave them time to explore. Sarah knew from Andrew's e-mails that he was intelligent and lighthearted, and that they had tons in common. As they talked that night, opening up more to each other about travel, favorite books and music, activities, family and background, they realized that they were incredibly similar. Both were the youngest of three children, with two older sisters each. Their fathers were highly literate men who had spent their formative years in Europe. Both fathers also had died of cancer at very young ages, and their mothers were admirably strong as they raised families on their own.

"My earliest suspicions were confirmed," says 40-year-old Sarah. "I knew he was my soul mate from the get-go."

The Self-Revelation Sequence

On their second date, Sarah and Andrew followed a sequence of self-revelation that psychologists say creates our most satisfying bonds with others. The sequence begins broadly then moves deeply, in this order: *shared interests* to *shared experiences* to *shared feelings*.

In step one of the sequence, Sarah and Andrew found common ground. On Match.com, 43-year-old Andrew wrote about his interests, ranging from in-line skating and camping to beer brewing and gourmet cooking. (When I first interviewed the couple, he was stirring a risotto while Sarah burped their six-month-old son, Henry.) Because of the online jump-start, their first two meetings were rich with likenesses and intriguing differences to talk about. There was breadth and harmony in their shared interests.

In step two, they exchanged more stories about their interests and found that they shared unique experiences. This harmony helped them to feel that they could trust each other. With the first roots of trust established, they reached step three, in which they went deeper and disclosed some shared feelings.

According to three decades of research by psychologists and other experts on love and marriage, nonintimate relationships progress to intimate relationships because of self-disclosure. (Google the words "self-revelation" or "self-disclosure," and you'll get tens of thousands of entries on the topic.) Internet dating accelerates the self-revelation process. That's why it's so important to understand it while you e-mail and when you first meet—and it continues to be important through all

THE WAY OF LOVE

As I researched self-revelation, it occurred to me that the traits psychologists discussed sounded very familiar. Then I remembered where I had heard them: in my own Protestant marriage ceremony. Here's the Bible passage from 1 Corinthians 13 (Revised Standard Version):

Love is patient and kind; love is not jealous or boastful; it is not arrogant or rude. Love does not insist on its own way; it is not irritable or resentful; it does not rejoice at wrong, but rejoices in the right. Love bears all things, believes all things, hopes all things, endures all things. ❧

the years of a marriage. Here are the qualities the research discusses. At its best, self-revelation is:

Patient. There is a tempo as well as a sequence to revealing the inner self. Your Internet introduction may make it tempting to disclose too much too soon. Resist the urge to blurt out everything at once. As in your e-mails, tell your story in good time. My friend Muriel Goldfarb, who has been married for more than 40 years, still surprises her husband with little gifts of herself. "How come you never told me this?" he asks. "Aah," she says, "I've been saving it for you." She's a wise woman who knows how to balance comfortable predictability and novelty.

Kind (and reciprocal). As one partner ventures to open up, it encourages the other to do so as well. And he will, if it feels safe. Sarcasm and hurtful remarks shut down the process. Be interested and sweet-spirited, not analytical or opinionated. Offer feedback with sensitive language that says you're listening and you care. "As you were telling me the story, I got a sense that . . . "

Modest. Self-revelation is not about being rudely boastful, arrogant, or aloof. It's really about a kind of self-confidence that doesn't need to show off.

Adaptable. Good self-disclosers are not stubborn in their attitudes. They don't insist on getting their own way, nor do they like only those who hold their exact same views. Although drawn to others who share their interests, experiences, and feelings, they accept differences that enhance a relationship. Sarah, for example, doesn't love to cook as much as Andrew does, but says, "I love to eat what he cooks." And she's fond of his quirky hobbies, like his new pastime, learning the accordion. "I'm so proud of our differences," she says. "He makes my life interesting."

Righteous. Women are more practiced at disclosing but not necessarily more clever at it. As girls we learn that showing our weaknesses ("I know I'm going to flunk algebra") or finding weaknesses in others ("Did you see what she wore to the prom?") is a good way to make friends. It may take a bit of work, but it's wonderful to unlearn those lessons and to rejoice, modestly, in the right things—what's strong and positive and true about others and ourselves.

Truthful. Honesty is part of truthfulness. Closer to the core of self-revelation is to be genuine and authentic. It feels validating to live more fully as the true self.

Hopeful. Our old gossipy ways weaken us. Also damaging are those juicy tales we love to dish with girlfriends. Past affairs, old family secrets—all those skeletons in the emotional closet—can crowd out the room needed for optimism and tomorrow's dreams. Can you store the old stuff somewhere else for a while, or clear it out altogether?

Lasting. When self-disclosure is appropriate, reciprocal, and all the positive qualities above, it creates a relationship that endures. The most desirable companion in life is someone who knows us broadly, deeply, and truly—and values what he knows.

THE THIRD DATE:
Make or Break?

Dating experts suggest that this one can be the biggie: the fish-or-cut-bait date, as my grandfather would say. For me and for some of the other Internet couples I interviewed, the third date marked the point when the personal ads came down and the search stopped. We just knew.

"Our third date lasted four days," says Sarah. "I'd never felt such amazing joy in knowing another person, and I had been dating since I was sixteen. It was such a celebration to be with Andrew; very special and sacred."

The third date may be enough time to know how you feel. Try an activity you both enjoy. Was it more fun together? Does he bring out the best of your true self? Do you think you could dream the same dreams?

The next chapter discusses sexual chemistry. Chapter 12 tells how to move a relationship that feels perfect right from the start toward commitment. But if a relationship feels wrong and you've given it two or three good tries, stop messing with it. Move on so that you don't miss out on the person who is perfect for you.

"Don't settle for anything less than your expectations," advises Internet-dating success story Charlene Black. "You can find what you really want."

PART

Four

CLOSING ON COMMITMENT

HOW TO TELL IF A RELATIONSHIP
IS RIGHT FOR YOU

COUNTDOWN TO MARRIAGE—
YOUR COURTSHIP CALENDAR

CHEMISTRY
AND SEX

What about this thing called chemistry? Do you need that spark, that instant sexual attraction, in a grown-up relationship? Does it matter?

The answers are not easy, because it's not easy to detach chemistry from the feelings that become love. Chemistry changes with time and experience, but maybe not as much as you'd expect.

In our youth, we're biologically programmed to reproduce. We look for good genes in a possible mate, along with the ability to provide for our offspring. Reproductive-influenced chemistry for a 17-year-old girl, for example, is likely to be about a hot body and a hot car: muscles being a sign of a good specimen; the car, a symbol of status.

The biological imperative to reproduce, however, recedes over the years. Middle-aged women are not as swayed as teenagers are by six-pack abs and convertibles. But here's the tricky part: the psychological and sexual components of our chemistry wish list doesn't evaporate completely.

How do we take advantage of chemistry without letting its power completely determine our decisions? We don't want to make the same selections a 17-year-old would. Or, as a guy would say, we don't want our little head to do the thinking for the big head. There are two instances when chemistry is most problematic, and both are a matter of timing.

Wrongheaded choices. If you rush into physical intimacy, you'll lose some of the chase and intrigue that build toward commitment. And you may suffer from surrender syndrome. One of my Manhattan friends, Megan, made a little-head decision about a handsome, blue-eyed rambler. From the very first date, she knew Al would let her down, and he lived up to his promise, hurting her faithfully for two years. Megan is smart, pretty, and successful. She admits she's not even in love with Al. Once she'd surrendered to him, though, a combination of guilt and disbelief at her own poor judgment kept the momentum going. I think she gave him more and more chances in hopes that she could justify the original bad emotional investment. Like Megan, you're too old to be lectured to, but don't you think waiting makes sense?

Snap judgments. Many of the women who met their true match online say there was instant chemistry at their first face-to-face meeting. Some women, however, are slow to warm. It may require three, five, even ten dates or more to feel a glow, like it did for Mindy, a 45-year-old commercial real estate broker in Manhattan. She met Sam, her fiancé, on JDate.com, the hot site for Jewish singles. They hit it off right away. "We were so much alike it was bizarre," she says. "We were reading

---

MULTIPLE FIDELITY

Internet daters keep their options open. A common practice is to correspond with several men, as many as you can keep straight, and meanwhile scan for newbies. It's an efficient use of time that insures a thorough search.

When a couple meets and starts to date, it's still presumed that either one is free to search, correspond, and meet others. In fact, I encourage you, especially if you're rusty at dating, to get out and practice. It helps reactivate your latent charm and figure out your mate criteria.

Feelings get hurt, however, as soon as intimacy enters the picture. You or he may not understand why a lover's photo is still posted on a site. The search may be over in one of your minds, but not the other's. If you're close enough to have sex with someone, you should be able to communicate your expectations. Whether you opt for faithfulness or continue to play the field, partners feel more secure when there are no surprises. ↖

the same book, and both of us just happened to have seen an independent film about a mullet-tossing contest. If I told him I had raw food for lunch, he'd say, 'You're kidding. I ordered raw takeout last night.'"

Mindy thought she might have found her missing twin, but she didn't find that attractive, even though Sam was super-good-looking. "I put him in the friendship column," she says, "and we were absolute best friends for two years."

Sam graduated to the other column on a spring evening when he was consoling her over yet another one of her dating disasters. "He said, 'Come over here and get a big hug,' and when I felt his gentleness and strength surround me, it was one of those ta-da! moments. Liquid jelly."

On her way to getting engaged to Sam, Mindy had time to reflect on her earlier resistance: "My M.O. had always been to go for the physical attraction and chemistry. I still had the mindset of the popular college girl. And, you know, when you think that way, you let sex and attraction hide a lot of faults. Like, 'Gee, he's so cute. Maybe he'll find a job next week.'

"I wasn't only immature. I was deep-down scared. I knew what to expect when I let the physical lead my thoughts and emotions. I knew I'd probably get hurt, but it was a *familiar* hurt. Plus—and this took a while to figure out—I could hold my real self in reserve. Popular Girl was out there getting hurt, but real me—Smart Woman—was safe. I had her concealed.

"My reservation with Sam was that it was too much self to give up to one person. I'd never had a relationship, not even in my first marriage, which combined the social and sexual with the intellectual and emotional. I didn't know if I could give all. It felt too intimate to give anyone that piece of me, too."

These days Mindy and Sam are busy decorating their loft in Manhattan and planning their wedding. "It's not that hard. We have the same tastes precisely," she says, "and he helped me pick out my furniture when we were friends. Our stuff really goes together.

"We're happy from a deep emotional level," she continues. "From that fateful moment when I decided to let it all happen, we have *fully* enjoyed each other."

As Mindy learned, it may take a while for big-head thinking to prevail, as a dater takes into account shared values, mutual respect, and common interests on one side of the scale and pure physical appeal on the other. Again, waiting makes sense. Give a good guy at least three chances to enchant you.

Remember, you're at a hormonally hectic, chemically vulnerable age. That initial thrilling reaction is not necessarily a signal that a relationship is "meant to be." It may be true. I know I felt that way with Walter. But that magic feeling could just as easily mean "you sure know how to court trouble." Lack of instant attraction can also be a miscue. Maybe that special feeling is waiting to appear on your next date. In other words, whether chemistry is there or not is not the best forecast of a wonderful relationship.

HOW PERIMENOPAUSE/MENOPAUSE AFFECT SEX

Perimenopause, when women first experience symptoms of the change in life, usually begins two to three (sometimes up to eight) years before menopause. Menopause itself usually occurs between the ages of 42 and 58, most often around 51.

The myth used to be that sex stopped when menopause started. I might add that the myth may have originated because life itself often stopped when menopause started. Our female ancestors didn't live long past 50. Today, the life expectancy of an American woman is 79.5 years. On average, that's almost 30 years postmenopause to enjoy physical intimacy.

Myths die hard, however. Your cultural expectations and beliefs about menopause can exert influence on your libido. Some women fall into the misery-loves-company trap. If you're around someone who likes nothing better than sharing a night-sweats story, guess what? Her fears and dreads and old wives' tales about menopause and sexuality are going to get embedded in your mind, too. Studies show that American women are much more preoccupied with and whiny about menopause than women in cultures such as Mexico. Frankly, if you asked me to choose between my 39 years of weeklong periods every month versus my two years with about five episodes of night sweats and the agony of occasionally having to pull a sweater off, my vote is clearly with the señoras.

For those of us who lucked out with good hormones and positive expectations, the change can have an interesting effect. It's almost as if our bodies rev up and shout: "Last call for mating!" The happily married 40- to 60-year-old women I know report renewed sexual interest in their spouses. There's a second-honeymoon feel to their marriages, particularly as the nest starts emptying, and there's more energy for other things. And silver singles? Watch out!

"I've never seen anything like the desires of fifty-year-old single women," says Jim Fischer, now happily married to his online match, Stephanie. "I wouldn't call them sex maniacs, but they practically are. Very open-minded and up front about what they want. I'd get offers like, 'Let's skip the movie and go to bed.' This was absolutely the reverse from when I was dating in my late teens to early thirties. It's great!"

I agree with Jim. A renaissance of sexual energy is something to cheer about. After years of fatigue from raising a family or nursing an ailing marriage, renewed desire is a wonderful gift.

But what if sex is something you dread rather than enjoy?

DEEPENING DESIRE

We begin the quest as little girls. Thanks to centuries of hard-won victories, females can attain just about any career we set our sights on, run for president, travel the globe, or explore outer space. But we know the true adventure of our lives will be our love stories.

I send my three-year-old grand-niece beautiful pop-up books about mammals, insects, the stars and planets. As one of the original proponents of Take Our Daughters to Work Day, I know how important it is for girls to think about the larger world. My bug books, however, gather dust. "Gracie's really fascinated with the Sleeping Beauty story," her mother hints.

We're always fascinated with love and passion.

Yet we know so little about it.

Pat Davis, the 61-year-old president of Passion Parties—a sort of Tupperware party for the bedroom rather than the kitchen—says women are hungry for information about their bodies and the underpinnings of desire. The company's consultants are new-style intimacy educators, filling a niche vacated by busy physicians who rarely bring

CONTRACEPTION AND PROTECTION

Menopause is the day when a woman has stopped having menstrual periods for one year. The standard advice is to continue contraception for a year after that, even longer if menopause occurred before age 50 or if you have used hormone replacement therapy. Check with your doctor. "Change of life babies" do spring up.

Also insist that your lover use a latex rubber condom for protection. There are about 100,000 reported cases of HIV/AIDS in women over age 50. Many are survivors of infections contracted a decade or so earlier. Intravenous-drug users and partners of drug users figure into the mix.

But there are also straight arrows within those statistics: wives, for example, who never suspected that their husbands would cheat. "Viagra came along and woke the dead," said one community organizer in the *New York Times*. "Their husbands started having sex with younger women."

Condoms also offer protection from herpes or other sexually transmitted diseases. Get regular tests, too. Many mature women can't believe a sexual disease could happen to them.

up a patient's sex life. The consultants ask, inform, prescribe in a sense (see "Shopping for Satisfaction" on page 184), and they make house calls—to an average of 10,000 American homes each evening.

Sales have increased 50 percent per year for the last four years. Passion Parties have tapped into the hidden American Dream: to feel sexually fulfilled.

"Women, regardless of age, want to have a satisfying love life," says Davis. "We sometimes have three generations at a party in someone's home. Whether they're eighteen or eighty, the question they ask is the same: 'Sex isn't that exciting for me, what can I do?'"

As party-goers open up to one another and the facilitator, misconceptions are cleared up. Davis explains: "A consultant might say, 'It generally takes about twenty to twenty-five minutes of stimulation to experience arousal and orgasm,' and women are shocked and relieved. They thought something was wrong with them because it took so long." (Men, by the way, need only about eight minutes.)

One woman, according to Davis, announced at a party, "I don't have the orgasm gene. Neither did my mother or grandmother."

"We helped correct that," Davis says, "and gave her permission to have pleasure. Then we talked about how to push the right buttons."

As it turns out, there are three right buttons that may need to be pushed simultaneously for the O to go. Culture, as discussed, is significant. The attitudes and beliefs of your upbringing may be unhelpful and stifling. For example: "sex is dirty," "sex ends at menopause," or "we don't have orgasms in our family." Lack of support from your peers can be harmful, or a partner's cultural hang-ups transferred to you. Sex education may be the elixir you need. Read, research, or host a Passion Party yourself to correct the misleading lessons (contact passionparties.com).

The Physical Factor

The second button is physiology or biology. From perimenopause through postmenopause, you can expect decreases in the blood supply to the vagina and in estrogen levels. That may dampen desire, cause dryness, and the vagina becomes shorter and the lining more fragile. You may want to make a change in sex positions if an old standby doesn't feel as comfortable as it once did. Kegel exercises also help by keeping vaginal membranes thick and strong.

Regular exercise and nutrition play a positive role as well. Working out often increases natural testosterone to a sexy level and sends blood coursing to hot spots down below. Sound nutrition supplies the energy you need for vitality and the healthful ingredients to keep you looking

SHOPPING FOR SATISFACTION: LUBRICANTS, LOTIONS, MAGIC BUTTONS, AND POTIONS

"Where Every Day Is Valentine's Day" is the slogan of Passion Parties. As a single woman, it makes sense to keep that reminder in mind and to keep special ingredients for romance on hand. Pretty lingerie, mood music, and wine you already know. Here's some more serious sexy stuff.

Dry goods: Wetness in the vaginal area is a sign of arousal. Moisture is also preparation for an intimate encounter. (The vagina creates little sweat beads.) If menopause makes you drier than you used to be, you may want to try an over-the-counter vaginal suppository, like Replens, or a personal lubricant, such as the K-Y Warming Jelly. With a bit of aid at the beginning, your natural wetness may soon turn up.

Your skin yearns for moisture, too. Fragrant oils or beads in the bath are relaxing renewers. Apply lotion faithfully to give your body a smooth, sensual feel.

Mechanical maneuvers: The clitoris has more sensitive nerves per millimeter than any other part of the body. Some researchers believe that it is even larger than the penis, but much of its tissue is hidden within the pelvic region. Elusive though it is, there's little question that it's the gateway to pleasure for many women.

The number three best-seller at Passion Parties is the Button, an egg-shaped vibrator designed to stimulate the clitoral network of nerves. "It

your best. Taking good care of yourself allows your body to work at peak efficiency in all ways.

The other holistic remedy to rev up your sex drive and tone your sexual organs is to have orgasms (gee, that's too bad) through regular intercourse or masturbation. In this case, an old adage—use it or lose it—is true.

Helen Fisher, Ph.D., author of *The Sex Contract*, describes a marvel that is unique to the human female. Satiation-in-insatiation means the more orgasms a woman has the more she is capable of having.

adds a little extra to lovemaking," says Pat Davis, "or helps reacquaint a woman with feelings of desire."

Critics of vibrators warn that they can spoil a woman for regular intercourse. Also, excessive use may—and there is much debate on this—damage delicate nerves. On the other hand, what's a girl to do about satiation-in-insatiation?

If you've been diagnosed with genuine sexual dysfunction, check into the Eros Therapy device, a prescription product popularly known as the "clit vac." The suction action (don't try to do this on your own, guys) creates blood flow to the clitoral and vaginal region. Vasocongestion, increased blood flow, is right up there with mental expectations and wetness for high scores in the scoring category. Visit Urometrics.com.

Ultimate lotion potion. There's good reason Passion Parties have had enviable success. Their number one product, Pure Satisfaction, the crown jewel of the company, combines expectancy, a moisture gel, and a natural amino acid ingredient, L-arginine, that encourages blood flow for arousal. Pat Davis advises a morning application "to awaken that area and help you notice your interest during the day."

It could be the placebo effect, but I dabbed some on this morning as directed, and I can't wait to get off this laptop. ▸

Adding to the kitty: as the number of orgasms increase so does their intensity.

This awesome capacity may lie dormant if it's never tapped (about a third of women have never achieved orgasm), or if you're out of the habit of sex. Pat Davis suggests that you can be the catalyst for your own change.

"Even if you're not currently with a partner," she says, "get the responsiveness parts working. Become comfortable with your own body. Then, when you find someone, you can show him what works for you."

What about an alternative to the holistic approach? Where's *our* Viagra?

The same miracle plumbing that brought you satiation-in-insatiation appears to be too complex to reengineer with a simple pill. "We know that Viagra doesn't work in women," says Beverly Whipple, Ph.D., vice president of the World Association for Sexology and coauthor of *The G Spot.* "Women are not minimen," she states, in an interview on WebMD.com. "We're different at the biochemical level."

The company that makes Viagra announced that it was concluding its research of Viagra in women. So that ends that. Other drug hopefuls include hormone patches, antidepressants, or herbal remedies, such as those below.

⬆ The testosterone patch Intrinsa substantially increased sexual interest in women, according to several studies. But the participants had had their ovaries removed or were on estrogen therapy. It will be several years before trials will be complete on women without these conditions.

⬆ Estratest, a combination of oral estrogen and testosterone, was developed and FDA-approved to treat hot flashes. But it has been used "off-label," according to WebMD.com, to improve sexual desire. Note, however, that oral estrogens may increase the risk of heart attack, stroke, breast cancer, endometrial cancer, and blood clots in the lungs or legs. Male hormones, the other part of the combo, can increase the risk of liver cancer, and cause masculizing effects in women (deepening of the voice, unnatural hair growth, and decreased breast size).

✦ A small study of 66 women indicated that the antidepressant Wellbutrin might kick up the libido in some women, although this sunny bit of news may be the result of depression lifting.

✦ The dietary supplement AgrinMax appears to have a positive effect on women's libido and satisfaction with their sex lives, according to a double-blind, placebo-controlled trial reported on WebMD.com. The article warns, however, that any herbal ingredient should be checked out by your doctor. AgrinMax, for example, contains gingko, which can promote bleeding.

It's a prudent idea to ask your gynecologist about anything you're keen on trying, including other aids such as vitamin E vaginal suppositories and natural progesterone creams. Hormonal tests may be in order to figure out a treatment for menopausal complaints like severe night sweats and a level of desire that stubbornly refuses to budge. Be sure to tell your physician about all the medicines you take. Some very common ones, like Pepcid AC or beta-blockers, may decrease responsiveness as a side effect.

With a safe, FDA-approved drug still more fantasy than reality, it may be quicker and wiser to stick with the holistic tonics. And you still have that third button: psychology.

The Psychological Factor

The reason your sex drive may be in low gear is very likely to have a psychological component. That's good news in a way. Maybe all you have to do is think positively to bring back desire. Let's examine the proposition.

Cognitive Physiological Feedback Loop (CPFL) is a term used to describe the all-important link between mental arousal and the physical response. For men, this is often a no-brainer. He sees his erection, can't help but notice the feeling. The tom-tom to the cortex drums out the message: "It's time to have sex. Now would be good."

To say that the signal system for women is less efficient is an understatement. We have no obvious—conspicuous, one might say—visual clues. We may sense a tingle, a little throbbing, and a slight wetness. The signs of arousal are easy to miss. If we were good at reading them, ovulation kits wouldn't be a multimillion-dollar industry.

Because we're so bad at CPFL, we may not know what we're experiencing. Eileen Palace, Ph.D., director of the Center for Sexual Health at Tulane University, has conducted landmark studies that prove how lousy women can be at processing information about our desire.

In one study, Dr. Palace hooked women up to a biofeedback machine that measures sexual response. The women watched soft-porn films, but reported no turn-on, even as the instruments recorded the opposite.

In a sneakier experiment, she verified a placebo effect. Nonorgasmic women were shown an erotic film. This time researchers interrupted after 30 seconds to tell the women—falsely—that their vaginal blood flow had increased. Sure enough, they then truly became aroused.

The takeaway from Dr. Palace's work is not that we lie to ourselves about sex, but that we need to be more sensitive to our subtle clues. The new research, in fact, offers great hope.

Here's how to maximize the discoveries of the sex experts.

Deal with distractions. You may find it hard to move from "the stress of the day to the romance of the evening," says Davis. "Women who are stressed out don't want to make out."

A chief cause of stress is doing things you don't want to do. Examine your priorities. Learn to say no. Make sure you have downtime between work and home.

Police the past. Your ex-partner may have been a dud or made you feel like one. A change in men, or in your self-esteem, could interest you in sex again. Desire begins with feeling desirable. Your cultural history may also intrude. Say goodbye to all those negatives. Don't shut yourself off from future happiness.

Manage the moodiness. You're feeling romantic. Then all of a sudden one little thing goes wrong. It triggers behavior much like what Matt Ridley describes in *The Red Queen*: "Male scorpions lull females into the mood for sex at great risk to their lives. One false step in the seduction, and the female's mood changes so that she looks upon the male as a meal."

Overlook minor irritations. Stay focused in the moment.

Pay attention to pleasurable feelings. Sexual urges may be hard to read. Ignoring them when they do appear closes off the CPFL circuit. Fan the flame. Hold on to that spark of desire through a busy day. Visualize excitement. Keep reminding the brain that the body wants to have sex.

Activity adds ardor. Raising the heart rate, breathing, and muscle activity improves the body's arousal potential, according to other work by Dr. Palace. A date at the gym, therefore, could be more enticing than a candlelit meal. An action adventure movie, playful tickling, or sharing laughter also creates the heightened effect. See if you can move it in a passionate direction.

Expect excitement. Anticipating arousal can make it happen, as Dr. Palace's study of the placebo effect demonstrates. In fact, our expectancies are more powerful than researchers ever imagined. The cortex likes to anticipate what is going to happen and has the neurochemical wiring to do so. As science writer Sandra Blakeslee puts it, there are "a host of biological mechanisms that can turn a thought, belief, or desire into an agent of change in cells, tissues, and organs."

In other words, if you believe in your own desire and think about it ahead of time, your mind will go along with it and get the body to respond—just like the "cold" women in Dr. Palace's study who warmed up all of a sudden when told they were "hot." Not everyone can make that transition so easily. And, as discussed in chapter 3, not everyone wants to improve her sex life—or have one at all. But, if you do, polish up your self-talk. The brain will listen.

Chemistry and sex are powerful forces. They can be an important part of a relationship, because we feel closer to a partner who attracts and satisfies us. In addition, women who are comfortable with their sexuality and sex lives tend to be happier, psychologists say. Perhaps that's because we descend from a long, long line of reproducers, and enjoying sex fulfills a destiny. But there are many kinds of love stories, many types of romantic adventures. Choose the one that's right for you wisely and in good time.

Coming up: how to get to lasting commitment.

YOUR COURTSHIP
CALENDAR

Sarah, with you, I am more caring and more involved. You are open, thoughtful, patient and loving with me. You help me take joy in life. I love you and want you with me.

If you become my wife, I promise to be attentive and to continue learning about you. I promise to treat you with kindness, and to work with you as we build our commitment to each other. I promise to turn to you to share my joys and for comfort in difficult times. I promise to celebrate life with you.

Will you be my wife?

Andrew, you make me laugh and you make me think. You help me find joy, wonder, and sacredness in everyday things. You encourage me to be myself, while also inspiring me to grow. I stay with you because of what I know, and what I want to find out.

If you will be my husband, I promise to be kind, caring, and attentive. I promise to encourage your ideas and interests, to rejoice in your happiness, to share my life, my feelings, and my hopes with you. I promise to respect your individuality and to join you in seeking fulfillment.

Will you be my husband?

—Excerpts from the wedding ceremony
   of Sarah Hutter and Andrew Hess

Don't you want to find what Sarah and Andrew have? All humans do.

We yearn for a partner who is kind, caring, attentive, thoughtful, and a relationship that is joyful, respectful, and celebrates growth. We want communication, friendship, passion. We hope to be able to share our everyday concerns and our exciting dreams. This chapter will lead you there.

COURTSHIP CALENDAR

On Valentine's Day, four months after meeting him, I expected a small velvety box from Walter. I was so in love, and knew he was, too, so why wait to marry? As it turned out, his timetable for the little box, a year later, was a better idea. Although our commitment was there from the third date, our families needed to catch up with our breakneck pace, and we still had some things we needed to learn about each other.

Our schedule, from that first "hello" to "I do," isn't actually that far from the norm. A survey by Match.com found that Internet daters who find the right match tend to marry within a year of meeting. The typical Courtship Calendar may be something like this.

Month 1: The Infatuation Factor

As early as date three, you already may have a sense of your relationship potential, although there are always exceptions—like Mindy and Al's story in chapter 11—that need a lot more time. Feel optimistic if you notice these positive signals of infatuation and early attachment:

- You idealize him. Everything you learn about him is fascinating.
- The fascination is mutual. He's curious and wants to know more about you, too.
- He calls regularly and stays on the phone at least 15 minutes.
- He does not hesitate to make future dating plans. He's not vague or squirmy. He's really into you.

Fan the fire by staying upbeat and keep the flirting going. You need to nurse those first sparks into a passion.

Month 2: Finding a Friend

Those first few months together should be a time to enjoy the interests and activities you have in common. Shared fun will knit you together and reveal personality like nothing else can. As your camaraderie grows, slowly find out more. Ask questions that get to the character and values on your Must List. He passes the friendship test if:

- He continues to call regularly.
- He's eager to make plans.
- His focus is on you when you're together.
- He listens well.
- He makes you laugh.

Months 3 and 4: Is He a Keeper?

If you've gotten to this point—past the self-evaluations, the search, e-mails, and early dates—you've eliminated the unsafe dates and men with whom you have nothing in common. But there are still mistakes to make—the false positives. They test positive on most counts but have a negative side. Know these types:

The Self-Esteem Vacuum. He's attentive and caring. From that first e-mail he wooed you with vigor. It's not hard to like someone who goes out of his way to be agreeable. Beware if he's too eager to please or rushes into love. He may not be an obsequious villain in disguise, like the Dickens character Uriah Heap, but the fawning, lovesick softy still spells trouble. His regard for you is the opposite of how he views himself. You can tell by the way he walks that he's not proud of who he is. Or notice his talk: Does he put himself down while putting you on a pedestal? Your job, if you should be unlucky enough to fall for his compliments, is to get sucked dry by his endless unmet needs.

The Fixer-Upper. He's not a wimp like the SEV. In fact, he may be a manly man, confident or even cocky, but he needs work. The characters Jack Nicholson portrays are the archetype. Do you remember the famous line in *As Good As It Gets*—"you make me want to be a better man"? I know many women who loved those words. I wanted to throw popcorn at the screen and shout, "Watch out, Helen Hunt! This is not as good as it gets, and this nutcase is going to make your life miserable!" Who wouldn't want to be a better man if the man you were could barely leave the apartment? In *Something's Gotta Give*, Diane Keaton also accepts the mission of repairing a flawed Jack character. She helps the heel heal, and pins her hopes for the future on the pretty unlikely probability that a world-class philanderer can have a change of heart before his next coronary.

"Real life is too short to deal with a big Fixer-Upper," says my friend Ann, who had a do-it-yourself project for the 15 years of her first marriage. "There are three other scenarios with this type," she adds.

"In the first scenario, there are no real foundation problems with the guy," explains Ann. "He may be rough around the edges, but just needs some Spackle and paint from time to time. He's happy for the help and appreciates your maintenance and good taste.

"In scenario number two, you bought the ranch, when you really wanted a center-hall colonial. You keep trying to renovate. What you really need to do is move—or accept the ranch. The ranch can't change and shouldn't want to. He can be pretty cozy if you let him be.

"Finally, there's my own scenario: the money pit. You start work in the attic, and the second floor caves in. You tile the kitchen, and the bathroom springs a leak. You patch and shore up, nurture and mend, and just when you have him ready, he heads for the door and finds someone who really likes all the work you've done."

Unfinished-Business Man. This type of guy definitely wants a relationship. He's not happy being by himself. He's also clear about what he doesn't want—someone like his former wife or lover. In fact, he talks a great deal about what a mistake that was. Remember the work you did in chapter 1? Unfinished-Business Man could use some self-evaluation, too. While he may not have the self-esteem problems or flaws of the SEV or Fixer-Upper, he needs time to get over his anger and mistrust to discover what he truly wants. That is, if he can recover. Sometimes he can't.

For example, I dated a successful economist who was a great jitter-bugger and very sweet to me. His battles with his ex, however, were so petty that I couldn't be around such negativity. When he died unexpectedly two years ago, I felt terrible that he had wasted precious time. He should have danced more, instead of playing a game of who's right and who's wrong. The executor of his estate later told me that the will was filled with bitter codicils. He could never stop fighting.

The other unfinished business is with childhood. If you hear him say, "You remind me of my mother," it may not be a compliment. Psychologists say that we all have unconscious wishes to reconnect with a parent. Some of us try again and again to recreate that all-important early relationship with a different partner, in hopes of getting it right.

True love is between two whole people. The man who deserves your commitment should be fully and wonderfully formed. Not that there aren't areas in which you want to grow together, but at your age, you don't want the nonstop job of boosting him up, kicking him in the pants, or mothering him. This time around insist on an *adult*.

He, in turn, deserves acceptance. He has earned peace and respect. Either welcome the uniqueness of his experiences and rejoice in his individuality, or let him go. If you want to change a man, that's the tip-off that you really want a change of men.

Month 5: Fanning the Flames or Flameout

The man you've chosen is a complete adult who's attentive for all the right reasons. You find yourself daydreaming about him. If you're sexually intimate now, your daydreams may include sexual fantasies. Proceed *care*fully. Your intense feelings may be the foundation for abiding love, or you could be working yourself into a flameout. Abiding love is a combination of your powerful feelings and rational reasoning (see "Month 6" on the next page). A flameout is a passion that burns brightly but quickly goes out.

Take, for example, the case of 60-year-old Jan, who met 62-year-old Frank on a senior site. He was courtly and dependable. Every night that they weren't together, he called at 9:30 on the dot to wish her sweet dreams. After a decade of being a widow, she was flattered by his attention.

"Frank put a smile back in my heart," she says. "I went from granny to girlfriend, and I loved it."

Frank mentioned in his profile that he was sexually active, and that was quite true. "He chased me around the couch on our second date," says Jan. "He was something."

Eventually, Jan decided the timing was right. "I can only describe our lovemaking as overwhelming," she says. "I'd never felt anything so astonishing, not even with my husband, though I had dearly loved him. That first night I just cried in Frank's arms."

Jan's fiery feelings burned for a couple of months. "Then we were at a party, and he was very controlling when we danced. 'Jan, hold your shoulders up. Don't look down. Wait until I signal you.' He was a dance Nazi, and I realized he tried to control me in other ways. Like those calls every night. Very sweet, but he was also checking up on me.

"Well, as they say, the veil dropped. I am so very grateful to Frank for reviving me. I didn't know I even had such a passionate side. But that was it. I didn't want to see him again."

Flameouts happen to men, too. One minute he's in red-hot pursuit, the next he's icy-cool, and you're wondering what happened to change the temperature. What happened is that total idealization and ultra-emotion are flighty and hard to sustain. The first sign of a flaw, and he's out of there—usually gone for good.

Flameouts can be puzzling, whether you're the one who cools or the one who is left cold. But they're not a waste of time. Jan learned something essential about herself from Frank. Her soul wanted that little bit of wandering to find the missing piece it needed.

Month 6: Are You Right as a Couple?

This month is usually a turning point, a time when two people in love seriously evaluate their long-term potential as a couple. There's an abundance of research on happy relationships to help you gauge your potential. As best summed up, getting along is a balance between the rational and emotional, along with realistic expectations and hopeful expectations. Both sides of the scale are important.

Rational and Realistic Expectations

Sexual chemistry is that first hint of emotional connectedness. It's transcendent, ephemeral, and glorious. But try living on it. Down-to-earth, sustainable relationships need a concrete and conscious foundation. This is the reality checklist:

✓ **Shared interests.** The more interests you share, the more opportunities you'll have to enjoy each other's company and create happy moments. On the other hand, you can't depend on interests alone. Avoid the country-club couple syndrome characterized by too many activities and too little intimate communication.

✓ **Similar backgrounds.** I remember a business meeting when I was frustrated that an important issue was overlooked. "May I just raise my voice here to make a point?" I said. My Italian-American colleague turned to me and laughed, "You little WASP. Is that how you raise your voice? You should have grown up around my dinner table. THEN YOU'D KNOW HOW TO RAISE YOUR VOICE! And you gotta use your hands to make a point." It was a very funny moment. But it's not funny when two people view the world from opposite perspectives and their many differences create ongoing criticism and conflicts. Harmony is most often achieved, as the research makes clear, when there is similarity in education, intelligence, religion, ethnicity, and socioeconomic background.

✓ **Common values.** Your moral compass and his point the same way. Trust, honesty, faithfulness, and family, for example, are not negotiable for either of you. You both also believe in going to church, voting for moderate candidates, and recycling. Or not. It's the congruency of values that seems to be important.

✓ **Money match.** Couples who are better off financially do seem to buy themselves out of a lot of trouble. They tend to rate themselves as highly satisfied with their relationships, perhaps because they can skirt the poorer folks' fights over spending, saving, and just squeezing by. Without questioning him like an accountant, you may want to probe his feelings about things like credit-card debt or retirement savings. Differing financial views can be daily sore spots.

✓ **Vital signs.** Do you have the same zest levels? Are your internal clocks, or biorhythms, in approximately the same time zone?

I know a couple at odds with each other in how they begin each day and spend every minute. He bounds out of bed; she lolls. He zips off to work; she needs time with her coffee and paper. Soon as he's home, he takes off again to jog or volunteer; she unwinds with the news and a cocktail. "I wish I could interest you in running," he complains. "I wish I could get you to chill," she snaps.

When a couple's biorhythms are off-kilter, they never see each other at their best. She sleeps through his wonderful morning moods. He misses her midday charm when she's finally awake and smiling. In addition, when energy levels are mismatched, there are fewer chances to have fun or enjoy each other sexually. Sex and recreation are the best stress-relievers, and they recharge the bonds of intimacy.

Emotional and Hopeful Expectations

A couple can check off every item on the rational/realistic list. That may be enough to keep them together. Being rational certainly makes sense. But when the heart also has buy-in, good relationships become great ones.

✓ **Positive affect.** This is a term psychologists use to describe a potpourri of good feelings, a mix of ingredients like humor and fondness. Have you shared a real belly laugh? Does a smile come to your face when you think of how silly he can be? Are you so fond of him that he qualifies as your best friend?

Liking someone this much only happens when there's mutual respect and acceptance. Actually, you must not only accept each other as is—without any fixing up—but also embrace the separateness, seeing it as an anchor for the relationship. As Sarah, in the chapter opening, vowed, "I promise to respect your individuality."

Affection also powers the positive. Therapists say they can tell if a couple will survive marital difficulties by noticing how they sit and touch during counseling. If there's affection, there's a chance

It's been six years since our first date, and my husband and I still can't keep our hands to ourselves. If he walked into my study right now (and I wish he would), we'd kiss, touch, say a sweet word, then get back to work.

Positive affect is that reservoir of goodwill that forgives, nurtures, winks, smiles, and wants you to come out and play. Deep friendship, good humor and fun, acceptance and affirmation, expressing and displaying affection are absolutely essential, according to the experts.

✓ **Romance and passion.** In the romantic beginning of a relationship, we idealize the one we love, viewing him as special and flawless. The feelings we experience are overpowering, as if we're truly under a spell, as Jan was with Frank. It's hard to sustain the crush phase. Some experts give it six months to last; others, up to two years. Eventually real life intrudes. But the spell doesn't have to be completely broken. Romance doesn't have to be a flameout. It can be the starting point for a long-term, passionate relationship and a place to return to refuel your sexual interest.

Couples that rate well on realistic expectations still express dissatisfaction if romance and sexual intimacy are lacking. Successful relationships are ones in which partners are as in sync about passion as they are on such mundane matters as whether to pay off a credit card.

✓ **Communication.** For decades researchers have pointed to communication as one of the best predictors of marital success. The basis of good communication is the ability of each partner to self-reveal and to respond to revelations from the other partner in an empathetic way. When a man or woman begins to hide or clam up about parts of the inner self, good talk and intimacy break down. Superficiality, and even deceit, may take over. Remember the statistic I cited in chapter 9: The average married couple lies to each other in one out of 10 interactions.

Communication stays honest and strong when we're able to express the things we're proud of as well as the things we're nervous about. Sometimes we want a cheerleader; sometimes we want someone to comfort us. But always we want an accepting, unconditional listener.

✓ **Encouragement.** Europeans call the ages from the late 40s to early 70s "the Third Age." The First Age, they say, is for learning; the Second Age, for working; the Fourth Age, for aging. The Third Age has the best job of all—the Third Age is for *living*.

This age can be a period of remarkable creativity, optimism, and energy. Mature adults can be as passionate about fulfilling dreams for the future as college freshmen, and can bring more experience and determination to the task. Maybe the goal is to change careers or change locations. Often there are multiple things you want to do—take up the cello, hike the Grand Canyon, tie flies like the artist John Kenrick. And, to put it bittersweetly, you want to squeeze everything in while you can.

As you live fully, you want a partner who cares enough about your happiness to share the risks and growing pains along with the pleasure and rewards.

Online dating allows you to choose from both sides of the ledger. As soon as you complete and send a questionnaire, you can screen for your practical requirements. Correspondence and early meetings fill in the blanks on the emotional side. You can come very close to the perfect match.

Month 7: The First Fight

You made a selection based on compatibility, and you've found someone with whom you have an amazing amount in common. There are, however, two individuals within the couple, and differences will emerge. In an accepting, empowering relationship, the separateness can be stimulating and attractive—most of the time. Conflicts inevitably arise.

That is especially true in the juncture between idealization and commitment. At this stage an inner voice starts whispering, "Do I want to put up with *that*?" How you work through to an answer is very important.

In just about every long-term study of marriage, how problems and conflicts are resolved is a key determinant of satisfaction. In the heat of an argument, if you can listen even when it's something you don't want to hear, and talk in a civil way even if you're expressing anger, problems will not grow out of proportion or fail to get resolved.

Learning to fight constructively is one of the hardest but most loving things you can do. Here are a few things that make it tough:

Who's fighting? There are many selves, many dances within a relationship, according to Douglas and Naomi Moseley in their book *The Shadow Side of Intimate Relationships*, and they parallel our family dynamics. You may take on a mother role and scold a man as if he were a boy. You might also try out the daughter part and be compliant as a daddy type tells you what to do. It gets tricky because you can switch personas mid-fight. If the daughter in you gets pushed too far, for example, you might send out the mom in you to battle for a while. In the meantime, he's shifting between father and son, dominant and wimpy.

Be in touch with signals that the mature adult inside you isn't present at the moment. You'll know your better side is off duty if:

- Your tone of voice changes. Do you sound like a loud, bossy mommy or a quiet little girl?
- You feel very anxious, not in control.
- Your partner is agitated or withdrawn.

Take a time-out and evaluate your feelings. Don't lose or bury them, but see if you can express them in a better way, using the tips that follow.

Start with you, not him. Quarrels often begin when you think: *If he would only change X, then I would be Y.* It's hard to see one's own complicity in a clash, but pointing a finger at him leads to defensiveness and creates a shell around his feelings. Better, say experts, is to switch the pronouns: *I feel X when you do Y.*

Listen. How do you react when the tables are turned, and he observes something about you he'd like changed? Do you see it as criticism or as a favor? To him, it's a favor: "Aren't you glad I'm pointing this out? I know you'll want to change it." To you, it may seem like criticism: "What do you mean? You're not so perfect, either!"

Everyone's sensitive to and terrified of change, and we get more stubborn as we age. "I'm too old to change," we justify, shortchanging ourselves of an unforeseen gift and opportunity to grow. No, you don't want an extreme makeover. You should not be someone's Fixer-Upper, just as you should avoid fixing someone up. But all of us have a zone in need of improvement, and someone who's brave enough to point it out *is* doing us a favor and paying a compliment. It's a favor to know how others perceive you or your actions, especially if someone's sharing a bit of truth about you in a well-intentioned way. It's a compliment, too, because it says, "I'm going out on a limb here, but I think you're strong enough and wise enough to want to be better."

Even more important, someone who is willing to explore your difficult parts and reach accommodation is headed for the deeper waters of commitment. Fighting the good fight indicates that you're "ready to risk a clearer, more realistic picture of a partner," say the Moseleys. It's a sign that you're willing "to go all the way."

When partners can give and take criticism and anger in an open, positive way, their relationship stays energized because they're fueling up below surfaces, tapping into the reservoirs of their inner selves. There's that rapport cycle again—self-revelation, acceptance, commitment. And when those real, sometimes uncomfortable feelings get blocked or stonewalled, the honest and true selves hide. That's when we become moody, distracted, sarcastic, and nutsy.

Pick a leader. I clearly remember my first argument with Walter because it has become an interesting metaphor for our relationship. I was used to slow, dependable public buses. He'd been battling bridges, tunnels, and city traffic for 25 years in his commutes. One evening, as he took me back to Manhattan after a weekend in the suburbs, his driving was so aggressive it scared me. At one point, he got out of the car in the middle of Central Park Drive and had words with the cab driver who was tailgating us.

When we got to my apartment, I said, "Look, I felt really scared. I didn't sense that you cared about my safety. I need to think about being with you."

He called when he got back to New Jersey and said, "I want to talk about this some more. Can I come back over?"

For hours that night we talked about more than how to merge lanes. Walter is a powerful man. That's what attracts me. But I knew he would be the lead driver in the relationship. Could I trust him in control?

That was such a difficult question. I was the oldest of five children, and like many kids who need to mature quickly for one reason or another, control was my issue. I felt anxious whenever I couldn't prepare, protect, and make my life safe. How could I compromise and cede power?

Control can be a real power struggle in many relationships. (And don't I know it! I've wrestled with it from both sides in two marriages.) But there are two very interesting things to know. First, if you can figure out the top dog—man or woman—ahead of time, you can save nine million fights about who's the boss. If one person needs to make decisions more than the other person, and does so, a relationship is more likely to continue than if both want to dominate or both refuse to decide, according to psychologists.

Second, if the alpha person isn't constantly challenged, she or he can be a wonderful listener, open to suggestions, willing and grateful to share power.

That first fight, for example, showed that Walter was willing to make a round-trip in peak weekend traffic to listen to my side. These days, if I observe that I'm feeling overpowered, he encourages me to push back, and I do. He wants me to feel safe with him.

A good fight will teach you rare information about a person, yourself, and your relationship. While the advantage of online dating is to minimize disagreements, when they do pop up, handle them with skill, maturity, and fairness, and be proud that you care enough to tackle the tough stuff.

Month 8: Are We Dreaming Together?

You've talked about personal goals. Your partner is encouraging and excited for you. But how will your dreams merge? Consider:

✓ **Harmony of interests.** I hope you already selected for shared interests. But plan a vacation together to see where you stand. If he's thinking wilderness camping while you think luxury cruise, see if this is a promising area of compromise or a promise of misery. The retirement years are noted for leisure pursuits—much more fun when pursued together.

✓ **Timing.** Is he ready to buy that fully loaded RV, while you still have 15 years to go on the corporate ladder?

✓ **Money.** What if you did eventually start your own company . . . Think you can count on him for support? Would you dig into your savings to finance a cross-country move?

✓ **Emotional support.** If he takes up the cello, will you mind the practice time? If you need help with your business plan, will he come through for you?

Discover now if you can meet the future with a partner who shares and commits to your dreams (and whether you can commit to his, too).

Month 9: Together Is Best

Do you feel lucky to have found each other? Do you feel more interesting, stronger, richer, more caring in each other's presence? Do you miss him deeply when you're not together? You've reached the milestone when you're sure together is best. You'll always want to be together.

Month 10: The World Intrudes

Friends and family have special radar to detect a serious relationship. Maybe your nonstop smile is a giveaway. In any case, the jig is up. They've discovered you're in love.

It's simpler to forsake all others and cleave only unto him when you're in your 20s. You're more than ready to leave Mom and Dad, and they're not too sad to see you go, either. When you're older, however, you may *be* Mom (and Dad), and feelings are more complex.

The standard advice is not to introduce children to someone you're dating until you're sure of your own feelings. I think that's very sensible, whether your children are young or grown. Emotions run high whenever a mother makes a step in an independent direction. It sets off alarms in an offspring's attachment-fear centers. You're *the rock*—and rocks aren't supposed to change or move.

Friends have their own attachment issues. Will you still have time for them? Will they get along with him? When you're absolutely sure of your own feelings, it's easier to be generous and available to others. From a calm center, you can reach out and be reassuring.

For example, Pam and Michael Pierre, from chapter 7, married one year and two weeks after their first date. At first, Pam's 24-year-old daughter, Latasha, gave her a hard time about the relationship. Pam kept her composure: "I knew she would come around if I was patient and let her know she was still my girl and very important to me. One day, she took a deep breath and said, 'If Michael can make you this happy, then I'm happy for you.'"

In my experience, family and friends can sense when a relationship is solid and good for you. Slowly sometimes, but surely, they welcome a joyous change.

Month 11: Commitment

In the early phase of a relationship, you can judge commitment simply by his presence. If he wants to see you and doesn't hesitate to make plans to be with you, he's announcing his intentions: I'm here, therefore I care. As you wind your way through the checkpoints in the Courtship Calendar—a disagreement or two, future plans, and family issues—you arrive at clarity: together is best.

Some men, as soon as they're sure of their feelings, easily make the leap to the next phase—lasting commitment. Others, however, need more time before they bring up the M-word.

More time and maybe some prompting. Although I didn't hound Walter about marriage after that first disappointing Valentine's Day, let's say that the word was out on the table. He knew that if he was going to be the center of my life, he had to be my husband.

John Molloy's research in *Why Men Marry Some Women and Not Others* reflects my experience. More than three-fourths of future grooms say they proposed because they were in love but also because the bride-to-be conveyed the message: *I'm the marrying kind, and I'll expect a proposal.*

Sarah Hutter describes herself as "cornier and more mainstream" than Andrew. It took some convincing after two years of dating to convert him from his free-spirited bachelor ways.

"Sarah and I visited Amsterdam over Christmas," Andrew says. "It was very romantic. We took a boat ride along the canals and had drinks at a small neighborhood bar. We started an emotional talk about our future, and before long we were in an impassioned argument that lasted until the early morning. The next day we both felt raw, vulnerable, and shaken. But as we walked the canals and talked about the night before, I was touched by how Sarah reached out to me, helping us reconcile our feelings and become closer. I felt a strong sense of trust in her and in our ability to work through whatever we might face in the future. I asked her to marry me."

Nine months, according to Molloy, is the point when most couples know if a relationship is meant to be. Most proposals or understandings occur about that time or a year or so afterward.

THE FUTURE

Ten years from now, researchers will have had a chance to conduct long-term studies of marriages that began as online relationships. Their findings, I'm sure, will be fascinating.

Marriage traditionally has been confined by geography and luck. You know the old plot lines: Boy marries girl next door; boy meets girl at college mixer; blind dates fall blindly in love. Half of these love stories work out. What will happen as we transcend geography and make our own luck?

Internet dating offers better odds at the get-go. You can select carefully and widely for the factors that researchers say create successful relationships. You don't have to look next door to find a person who shares your background and values. I found my Southerner, for example, in the Yankee state next to mine. You don't have to confine your search to someone who shares a single interest with you. You may share a dozen, and each creates a touch point of closeness.

Besides broadening and enriching choices, the Internet gives daters a chance to start out in a mode of self-revelation. You're more open and real out of the gate, which sets in motion the kind of communication that matters in a relationship: two true selves revealing, affirming, connecting.

With such a bright beginning, it's easy to see why the online daters I interviewed from all parts of the country—Oregon, Ohio, South Carolina, New Hampshire, New York—make the identical claim: I found my soul mate.

I wish you that same blessing.

POSTSCRIPT

March 22, 2005

It's a beautiful, sunny Spring day. My husband and I are playing golf on a resort course in Fairhope, Alabama. I hit a lucky shot that lands inches from the water—a perfect lay-up. Walter hugs me in congratulations.

A handsome man in his late fifties, who'd been watching on the other fairway, zips by on his golf cart. "I need one of those," he shouts. I think he's referring to my lay-up until he continues. "Where do I find a buddy like that?"

"On the Internet," Walter yells back, and pulls me even closer.

APPENDIX

TOP 10 MATCHMAKING ACTIVITIES

Activities are an important part of the online dating process. In the profile and questionnaire, you'll be asked what you like to do. Activities also are heavily weighted in the search (see chapter 7). You'll seem more energetic, fun to be with, and interesting if you're out and about. Who knows? You could also meet someone this way.

Before you fill out anything or take up a new interest, do some strategic thinking. What sports offer the greatest chance of companionship? If you've got a lot of gumption, you may want to pick a popular pastime that abounds with men. I have two women friends who tried shooting sporting clays, for example, and are now avid fans. Men flock to their sides when they talk about their scores at the various stations. My friends love the sport and love the attention. On the other hand, if you're as uninterested in taking up arms as I am, there are many, many other options.

To narrow down the choices, I reviewed a survey of sports participation commissioned by the National Sporting Goods Association. The study used a representative sample of 6,800 households. You can draw your own conclusions, but here's how I evaluated recreation for matchmaking potential, keeping four criteria in mind:

Number. There are fabulous sports like sailing or skiing that need water or snow to be really amusing. As a consequence, their numbers are weaker, especially in the 35-to-64 age groups. The Top 10 Matchmaking Activities have at least two million midlife male devotees.

Gender advantage. If you, like my friends, want a field of men to yourself, nothing can beat guns and bows and arrows. The tamer sports that I'm fond of aren't nearly as advantageous. No doubt you know this already. How many guys do you see in your aerobics class—the instructor? There are 72 percent more women than men your age in a typical class. You need aerobic exercise, of course, but don't count on it as mate bait. Gender-advantaged sports get bonus points on the Top 10 list.

True devotion. Men who are into muzzle loading outnumber women by 83 percent. But before you drop out of step class and pick up a musket, consider frequency. You'll catch him swapping shots only 10 times a year. That's hardly enough to get fired up about. If mature guys are not practicing the sport an average of at least 20 times a year, it's off the list.

Longevity. Here's something else to think about. An interest such as weight lifting is appealing at first glance—large numbers of men, good gender ratio, and true devotion (91 days a year). But if you picked up this sport, by the time you got really good at, say, bench-pressing, he'd be over it. There's a rapid rate of decline in participation for weight lifting, mountain biking, wilderness camping, hiking, skiing, and tennis. Sports on the Top 10 list keep men engaged through age 64. Sports with more than a 50 percent rate of decline lose points.

So, what are the best sports?

1. Golf. I would have picked this based solely on my personal opinion, but the stats prove me right. With 69 percent more midlife men than women playing, golf offers a substantial gender advantage. You'd have to pick a munitions sport to get better odds. The 32 days of participation ranks golf right after fitness activities, such as weight lifting, and ahead of all other recreational sports. These 9.4 million male fans are devoted, and they're devoted for a long time—only exercise walking stays a better course to age 64.

2. Exercise walking. You lose the gender advantage—32 to 42 percent more women than men—so make sure you get some really cute walking clothes to stand out from the crowd. You can't argue with the frequency (103 days) and longevity of this activity, however. Plus, the numbers are huge—over 14 million men ages 35 to 64.

3. Fishing (salt and freshwater). There are just over 12 million mature male anglers. The gender advantage—58 percent—makes it easier to hook one. Participation (20 days) and longevity put it right in the middle of the pack.

4. Bicycling. Riders are devoted. The 6.5 million male bikers ages 35 to 64 put mettle to the pedal an average of 57 days a year, and there are 20 percent more of them than women bikers. Numbers glide downhill, however, after age 55.

5. Hunting. Hunters ages 35 to 64 outnumber cyclists by about a million men. The gender advantage is also exceptionally high—88 percent more men. Hunting with a bow and arrow has a slightly better gender advantage—89 percent more men—but fewer numbers (just over 2 million). Bicyclists, however, participate in their sport nearly three times as often as hunters do, at just 20 days.

6. Swimming. On the plus side, 7.2 million men ages 35 to 64 swim an average of 36 days a year—that's almost twice as many days as men set aside for bowling, fishing, or hunting. On the minus side, the enthusiasm doesn't last forever. The rate of decline in participation is 39 percent after age 44, and another 47 percent decline after 55. It's also hard to get past the gender disadvantage—by ages 55 to 64, 24 percent more women than men are in the pool. Do you look *really* great in your suit?

7. Working out at a club. There they are—nearly 5.5 million men ages 35 to 64 on treadmills, stationary bikes, and rowing machines, 157 days a year. But they're surrounded: on one side by the 26 to 30 percent more women than men in the mature age group—and on the other side by more than 6 million women ages 19 to 34.

8. Target shooting. If you set your sights on a marksman, you sure don't have to worry about other women of any age. In the 35-to-64 age group, there are 68 percent more men than women—5.3 million male straight shooters practicing 23 days a year.

9. Bowling. The 2 percent gender gap gives you a slight advantage if you want to strike up a relationship with one of the 6 million–plus male bowlers ages 35 to 64. But catch him when you can: Men head to the lanes an average of only 20 days per year, and there are steep declines in participation after age 44. Bonus points for the gender advantage keep it (barely) on the list.

10. Running. Devotion is tops. The 3.8 million male runners ages 35 to 64 keep up the pace 211 days a year. Then their knees must give out or something because the rate of decline is swift—a 47 percent drop after age 44; a 56 percent downturn between ages 55 and 64. But the gender advantage—26 percent more men than women—could make the chase interesting for a while, and it keeps running on the list.

Other Good Sports

If you're not game for any of these sports, don't fret. The list is merely something to think about. Your interests certainly don't have to merge with a man's, although it could be fun if they did. What's really important is a commitment to fulfillment and personal health. In an annual survey of Boomers conducted by Harris Interactive, 70 percent of respondents concluded that they will live longer and be happier if they remain physically lively. There's no wrong activity if it gets you in motion. How about square dancing, salsa, kayaking, scuba diving, rock climbing, martial arts, river rafting, or pickle ball?

RICHER SPORTS

These activities attract the most men (ages 35 to 64) with average household incomes of $75,000 or more:

Exercise walking	25,293
Swimming	18,606
Camping	14,470
Bowling	13,290
Biking	13,276
Golf	12,467

Working out at a club	11,786
Boating	8,968
Target shooting	4,760
Downhill skiing	4,000
Waterskiing	1,836
Cross-country skiing	954

HOW WE PLAY

These are the top activities for men and women ages 35 to 64. The list is arranged by the highest number of male participants.

Activity	Male Participants	No. of Days/Year	Female Participants
Exercise walking	14,424	103	24,517
Fishing	12,035	20	5,048
Camping	10,402	14	9,579
Golf	9,465	32	2,870
Hunting	7,488	20	928
Swimming	7,246	36	8,942
Billiards	6,931	21	3,657
Bicycling	6,520	57	5,184
Boating	6,413	18	4,458
Bowling	6,280	20	6,172
Working out at a club	5,482	157	7,674
Hiking	5,418	15	5,035
Weight lifting	5,312	91	3,653
Target shooting	5,296	23	1,655
Running	3,861	211	2,811
Backpacking	3,004	14	1,824
Aerobic exercising	2,662	98	8,979
Bow hunting	2,173	15	233

Activity	Male Participants	No. of Days/Year	Female Participants
Mountain biking	1,843	16	667
Downhill skiing	1,787	28	1,296
Muzzle loading	1,581	10	266
Tennis	1,339	27	1,381
Waterskiing	1,122	11	607
Archery	1,110	21	295
Sailing	633	15	475
Cross-country skiing	626	19	483

Sports with More Men than Women (By Percentage)

Bowling	2
Camping	7
Hiking	7
Bicycle riding	20
Cross-country skiing	22
Sailing	25
Running	26
Downhill skiing	27
Boating	30

Sports with More Women than Men (Percentage More/Age Group)

	35–44	45–54	55–64
Aerobic exercise	72	69	69
Exercise walking	43	44	32
Working out at health club	27	30	26
Swimming	16	21	24
Tennis	9	21	42

Many More Men than Women (Percentage More, Ages 35 to 64)

Weight lifting	31
Backpacking	39
Waterskiing	46
Billiards	47
Fishing	58
Mountain biking	63
Target Shooting	68
Golf	69
Archery	73
Muzzle loading	83
Hunting	88
Bow hunting	89

True Devotion
Mean No. of Days of Participation
(Men Ages 35 to 64)

Running	211	Bowling	20
Working Out	157	Fishing	20
Exercise walking	103	Hunting	20
Aerobic exercising	98	Cross-country skiing	19
Weight lifting	91	Boating	18
Bicycling	57	Mountain biking	16
Swimming	36	Bow hunting	15
Golf	32	Hiking	15
Downhill skiing	28	Sailing	15
Tennis	27	Camping	14
Target shooting	23	Backpacking	14
Archery	21	Waterskiing	11
Billiards	21	Muzzle loading	10

Long-Term Prospects

	Percentage Rate of Decline, Men 35–44, 45–54	Percentage Rate of Decline, Men 45–54, 55–64
Mountain biking	63	49
Tennis	61	9
Downhill skiing	55	48
Weight lifting	51	65
Running	47	56
Backpacking	46	62
Billiards	43	62
Aerobic exercising	42	60
Hiking	42	38
Bowling	41	57
Working out at a club	41	48

	Percentage Rate of Decline, Men 35–44, 45–54	Percentage Rate of Decline, Men 45–54, 55–64
Swimming	39	47
Sailing	37	+17
Muzzle loading	37	40
Bow hunting	37	45
Fishing	35	36
Camping	34	50
Bicycling	33	48
Archery	31	79

Better:

Water skiing	28	65
Boating	26	35
Hunting	25	37
Golf	21	34
Target shooting	20	44
Exercise walking	16	23
Cross-country skiing	11	72

SOURCE: Statistics adapted from January 2004 survey of sports participation commissioned by the National Sporting Goods Association.

REFERENCES AND SOURCES FOR FURTHER INFORMATION

Baker, Anita. 2002. "What Makes an Online Relationship Successful? Clues from Couples Who Met in Cyberspace." *CyberPsychology and Behavior* 5, no. 4.

Barker, Olivia. 2003. "No Time for Dating?" usatoday.com. Quote from Barbara Dafoe Whitehead.

bbhq.com. "Boomer TV: The Stuff We Watched" and "The BBHQ Online Boomer Top 100."

Berger, Leslie. "The Ten Percent Solution: Losing a Little Brings Big Gains." *New York Times*, June 22, 2003.

Blakeslee, Sandra. "Placebos Prove So Powerful Even Experts Are Surprised." *New York Times on the Web*, October 13, 1998.

Bureau of Justice Statistics, U.S. Department of Justice. ojp.usdoj.gov.

cinepad.com. "The 100 Most Acclaimed Movies of All Times."

Clark, Carolyn Chambers. "Exercise Away Menopause Changes." bellaonline.com.

comscore.com. ComScore Networks/Online Publishers Association. Statistics on personals.

Conru, Andrew. Telephone interview, September 2004.

couplescompany.com. "Singles Over 50: Women Want More Sex: Men Want Common Interests."

Cooper, A., and L. Sportolari. 1997. "Romance in Cyberspace: Understanding Online Attraction." *Journal of Sex Education and Therapy* 22:7–14.

Cox, Tracey. 2003. *Superflirt*. London: Dorling Kindersley.

Davis, Pat. Telephone interview, March 2005.

Del Webb. 2003. "Baby Boomer Report, Annual Survey." Survey conducted by Harris Interactive.

DePaulo, Bella M., and Deborah A. Kashy. 1998. "Everyday Lives in Close and Casual Relationships." *Journal of Personality and Social Psychology* 74, no. 1: 63–79.

———. "Cues to Deception." 2003. *Psychological Bulletin* 129, No. 1:74–118.

Dimensions. Newsletter of eHarmony.com.

Duenwald, Mary. "Over-the Counter Menopause Test Kits Offer Few Answers." *New York Times*, August 17, 2004.

Farid, Hany. Telephone interview, August 2004.

Firestone, Robert W. 1987. *The Fantasy Bond*. Los Angeles: Glendon Association.

Fisher, Helen. 1992. *Anatomy of Love*. New York: Fawcett Columbine.

Fowler, Jane. "Things You Should Know About HIV and Older Women." Hivwisdom.org.

Friday, Nancy. 2001 reissue. *Men in Love*. New York: Random House.

Gwinnell, Esther. 1999. *Online Seductions*. New York: Kodansha International.

Hardey, Michael. 2002. "Life Beyond the Screen: Embodiment and Identity Through the Internet." *The Sociological Review* 50, no. 4: 570–585.

Hendrick, Susan Singer. 1981. "Self-Disclosure and Marital Satisfaction." *Journal of Personality and Social Psychology* 40, no. 6: 1150–1159.

iVillage.com. The Perfect Partner Test.

Jones, Hilary. "Sex After the Menopause." netdoctor.co.uk.

Kashy, Deborah, A. and Bella M. DePaulo. 1996. "Who Lies?" *Journal of Personality and Social Psychology* 70, no. 5: 1037–1051.

livingto100.com. Healthspan calculator.

Mahoney, Sarah. "Seeking Love." AARPmagazine.org/lifestyle, November 7, 2003.

maturemarketing.com. "The Mature Market."

Marano, Hara Estroff. "The Reinvention of Marriage." Yahoo.com. (Originally published in *Psychology Today*, January 1992.)

McKenna, Katelyn Y.A., Amie S. Green, and Marci E.J. Gleason. 2002. "Relationship Formation on the Internet: What's the Big Attraction." *Journal of Social Issues* 58, no. 1.

McNeil, Donald G. Jr. "Facing Middle Age and AIDS." *New York Times*, August 17, 2004.

Merrick, Amy. "How Technology Has Changed the Way We Find Love." wsj.com, November 13, 2000.

Molloy, John T. 2003. *Why Men Marry Some Women and Not Others.* New York: Warner Books.

Moseley, Douglas and Naomi Moseley. 2000. *The Shadow Side of Intimate Relationships.* Sandwich, MA: North Star Publications.

Naimish, Carmen. InCase, "Date Detective." Tips from Web site and telephone interview with DateSmart.com founder. InCase and DateSmart are Registered Marks with the United States Patent and Trademark offices.

National Sporting Goods Association. 2004. Survey of Participation.

Nautilus Group. "Insights into the Baby Boomer Market." May 2002. (Results of commissioned paper by Yankelovich Partners, Inc., entitled "Yankelovich Monitor Perspective on Boomers.")

Northrup, Christiane, M.D. "Sexuality in Menopause: Finding Your Sexual Energy and Truth." drnorthrup.com.

Online Dating Magazine. "eHarmony Reveals Daters 'Must Have' and 'Can't Stand' Preferences." onlinedatingmagazine.com, July 19, 2004.

———. "Match.com Claims Their Marriages Are Successful." February 18, 2004.

Pastore, Michael. "Baby Boomers and Seniors Fastest Growing Web Groups." clickz.com, April 4, 2000.

PR Newswire. "Study Shows Marriages of Couples Who Met on Match.com are Happy, Romantic and Loving . . . " February 11, 2004.

Psychology Today staff. "An Arrangement of Marriages." Yahoo.com. (Originally published by *Psychology Today.* January/February 1993.)

Pugliese, John, Deborah Wilson-Ozima, Janice Botzbach, Lori Lynch, Natalie Saldana and Stanley B. Woll. 2003. "Age Difference in Self-Presentation in Internet Dating." Paper presented at Western Psychological Association convention, Vancouver, B.C.

Raley, Kelly. 2004. "Not Even if You Were the Last Person on Earth! How Marital Search Constraints Affect the Likelihood of Marriage." *Journal of Family Issues* 25, no 2: 167–181. And telephone interview.

Ridley, Matt. 2003. *The Red Queen: Sex and the Evolution of Human Nature*. New York: Perennial.

rpi.edu. 1988. Interview with Joseph Walther.

Schnedler, Marcia. "Boomers Crave More Action, Better Amenities." Universal Press Syndicate, August 9, 2003.

Sherman, Richard, Christian End, Egon Kraan, Alison Cole, Jammon Campbell, Jaime Klausner, and Zachary Birchmeier. 2001. "Meta-perception in Cyberspace." *CyberPsychology and Behavior* 4, no. 1.

Strassberg, D.S., and S. Holty. 2003. "An Experimental Study of Women's Interpersonal Ads." *Archives of Sexual Behavior* 32, no. 3.

Straus, Tamara. "Amour Online: Darwin Wouldn't Have Been Surprised." AlterNet.org, January 14, 2002. Interview with Anita Baker, Ph.D.

Suler, John. *The Psychology of Cyberspace*. Book published online. rider.edu/~suler/psycyber/psycyber.html.

Talk Magazine. Excerpt from *The Case for Marriage*. October 2000.

Travel Industry Association. 2003. Domestic Travel Marketing Report.

U.S. Census Bureau. 2000. "Marital Status of the Population by Sex and Age." Current Population Reports.

Walther, J.B. 1996. "Computer-mediated communication: Impersonal, interpersonal, and hyperpersonal interaction." *Communication Research* 23: 3–43.

Whitty, Monica, and Jeff Gavin. 2001. "Age/Sex/Location: Uncovering the Social Cues in the Development of Online Relationships." *CyberPsychology & Behavior* 4, no. 5.

Whyte, Martin. 1990. *Dating, Mating, and Marriage*. Chicago: Aldine.

Woll, Stanley. Telephone interview, August 2004.

womenof.com. "*The Case for Marriage*: A Conversation with the authors."

Young, Jeffrey. "Cupid's Arrow Flies Straighter in Chat Rooms Than in Bars, Research Suggests." chronicle.com, April 5, 2002.

Zamora, Dulce. "Revving Up Women's Sex Drive." WebMD.com, July 26, 2004.

Ziegler, Jeffrey. "Recreating Retirement: How Will Baby Boomers Reshape Leisure in Their 60s?" *Parks & Recreation*, October 2002.

INDEX

Underscored page references indicate boxed text.